John & Bob,

Thank you for living and leaving a Legacy of Life in all you are and do!

Warm Regards,

KAI-ZEN

BREATHING LIFE INTO LEADERSHIP

INGER ANDRESS

Kai-Zen - Breathing Life Into Leadership
Inger Andress

Published by Kai-Zen Solutions, Lutsen, MN

Copyright© 2014 by Inger Andress
All rights reserved.

This book, or parts thereof, may not be reproduced in any form without permission, except in the case of brief quotations embodied in critical articles or reviews. The scanning, uploading, and distribution of this book via the Internet or any other means without permission of the publisher is illegal, and punishable by law. Please purchase only authorized editions, and do not participate in or encourage piracy of copyrighted materials. Your support of the author's rights is appreciated.

ISBN: 978-0-9904533-1-4 (Print)
ISBN: 978-0-9904533-0-7 (E-Book)

((DEDICATION))

THIS BOOK IS DEDICATED
TO MY LOVING GOD
WHO BREATHES LIFE INTO ME
AND WHO WILL BREATHE LIFE
INTO THOSE WHO MAKE THE TIME
CONTEMPLATE,
AND IMPLEMENT
THE IDEAS THEY HAVE RECEIVED
FROM THIS BOOK

((CONTENTS))

INTRODUCTION	III
ONE--	
THE POSITION OF OPPORTUNITY	1
TWO--	
RELATIONAL INFLUENCES	17
THREE--	
THE CULTURE OF COMMUNITY	37
FOUR--	
IMPLEMENTING SMALL STEPS TO SUCCESS	53
FIVE--	
SUSTAINABLE ENERGY	79
SIX--	
THE EMERGENT LEADER	99
SEVEN--	
LEAVING A LEGACY OF LIFE	113
ACKNOWLEDGMENTS	125
BOOKMARK – CITATIONS	129

((INTRODUCTION))

WHEN I INTRODUCE LEADERS TO THE CONCEPT OF KAI-ZEN, I often start with this phrase: Humanizing the workplace for the wellbeing of all.

Kaizen is a Japanese word that literally means improvement. The kaizen philosophy has been applied across a wide spectrum of the business world—from healthcare to manufacturing—in an attempt to lean practices and continually improve all aspects of a business.

In my work as a leadership/business advisor, I've expanded on the kaizen philosophy to get at the core of what makes a leader in this twenty-first century successful. For me, kaizen starts with humanizing the workplace, re-energizing individual employees, and injecting the entire work culture with renewed vigor and forward momentum. When you break the word into two parts, I find you discover a deeper meaning that gets to the heart of what I hope to offer: Kai, a restorative and innovative change; and Zen, the peaceful good of all.

In this post-industrial age, we tend to focus on efficiency, productivity, and speed—all great things, but somehow not quite enough to sustain the life of a leader or the energy of his people. In an effort to lean practices, organizations have often unwittingly put primary value on employee output. People are left feeling like machines whose only value comes from the amount and speed at which they can produce. Sadly, and to our own detriment, we've lost focus on the humans doing the actual work. It is time to refocus on what drives and motivates people. Doing so will inspire employees from within, allowing them the opportunity to use their strengths, and giving them a sense of purpose and fulfillment. This not only results in a more engaged workforce, it is a strong influencer of overall organizational growth. People who feel valued are more engaged at work and in life. They are better able to be a positive force at work and better equipped to influence the world around them. I've seen this work. Through research, conversations with business owners, and my own work in the field, I have been convinced the Kai-Zen philosophy is transformative. Not only can it breathe life back into you, your employees, and your business, I believe it *will*.

You will find throughout this book that I will share some real-life stories that might not be business related, but instead are simply about people. I find these stories inspiring, and I believe they can teach leaders how to reach the heart of the twenty-first-century culture. One thing I ask is that as you read, you allow yourself to enjoy, relax, and contemplate the questions. What you are about to

INTRODUCTION

receive from this book is designed to add fulfillment to your life, but be patient, it might not show up until the last sentence.

The goal of this book is to help you as a leader—business owner, CEO, founder, lieutenant, doctor, manager, director, coach, teacher—start on this path toward a more humanized organization that breathes life into your people, and in turn will restore life into you as the leader. This will result in success for your company, but most importantly, the wellbeing of all.

NAMASTE

((CHAPTER ONE))
THE POSITION OF OPPORTUNITY

THE FULFILLED LIFE is aware of its passions and desires. Without this chemistry from within, life is viewed as work and work as life. The goal is to help find the part of you that instigated this journey of leadership and continue to move forward towards an entity that gives you life, and gives life back to the world. The desperation that develops when one misses this step brings a sense of being trapped within the walls of your work role. This will contribute to the shutting down of any vibrant energy and innovative thought in our daily lives. How do we prevent ourselves from getting to this point? How do we get out if we are already submerged? These are vital questions for the CEO, manager, doctor, teacher, director, coach, lieutenant, or founder to ask in order to understand what will breathe life into them while leaving a lasting legacy of life to those under their charge. This is where they will come to a crossroad of choice in this twenty-first-century style of leadership: whether or not to embrace what I call the Position of Opportunity.

In his March 15, 2014 *Forbes.com* article, "Why Companies Fail to Engage Today's Workforce: The Overwhelmed Employee,"[1] Josh Bersin states,

"Companies are struggling to engage our modern, twenty-first-century workforce." Bersin cites evidence from a 2014 Deloitte-Global Human Capital Trends study with 2,500 organizations in 90 different countries. Among the study's findings, 86 percent of business and HR leaders believe they do not have an adequate leadership pipeline, 79 percent believe they have a significant retention and engagement problem, and 75 percent are struggling to attract and recruit the top people they need. What is happening to leadership in this century? How are these alarming statistics going to be addressed? To pose it more poignantly, how can we make life more fulfilled and less fatiguing not only in ourselves, but also in the lives of others in the workplace?

Whether you're a CEO, founder, lieutenant, manager, coach, teacher, volunteer coordinator, etc., you are in a position to directly influence the quality of life of those under your leadership. It is more than simply knowing the names of your employees, or even genuinely caring about them as individuals. Your true Position of Opportunity is the unique ability as a trusted leader to facilitate others' strengths, ignite their passions, and spark what drives them so they can excel beyond their own expectations. We need to be willing to redefine the twenty-first-century leader to bridge the gap from old, traditional ways that insulated the position from the whole to transparent leaders who breathe life into the cultural facets of their company.

When I first meet someone, there's one question I usually get around to asking: What was your favorite job, and why? The answers are varied and always revealing, but a few key themes seem to rise to the top. Even if you stopped and asked yourself that question right now, before you continue reading on, what would your answer be? Would it include a boss that took the time to mentor you? Or, would it have some relational aspect with a co-worker whom you felt had your back, someone you could trust? Maybe, instead, it was a whole team effort where respect and community were allowed to grow, where your ideas were listened to and incorporated into an action plan for the company? My guess is that if you think back, your answer probably had some combination of the above ingredients, you probably didn't even mind working extra hours at that favorite job.

In most cases, a good job has infinitely more to do with the person-to-person interactions—where respect and community allow for a free and positive exchange of ideas—than the actual task. This is where the philosophy of Kai-Zen can be most helpful in putting these intentions into practice. I like to explain Kai-Zen as the humanizing of the workplace; re-energizing individual employees, and injecting the entire workforce with renewed vigor and forward momentum. When you break the word into two parts, you will discover a deeper meaning that gets to the heart of what I hope to offer: Kai, a restorative and innovative change; and Zen, the peaceful good of all.

In this post-industrial age, leadership tends to focus on efficiency, productivity, and speed—all great things, but somehow not quite enough to sustain the life of a leader, an organization, or the energy of its people. In an effort to lean practices, companies have often unwittingly put primary value on employee output. Employees are left feeling like a machine whose only value comes from the amount and speed at which they can produce. Sadly, and to our own detriment, we as leaders have lost focus on the people doing the actual work. It is time to refocus on what drives and motivates people. Doing so will inspire employees from within, allowing them the opportunity to use their strengths and giving them a sense of purpose and fulfillment. This not only results in a more engaged team, it is a strong influencer of overall organizational growth and engage the younger generation. People who feel valued are more engaged at work and in life. They are better able to be a positive force at work, and better equipped to influence the world around them.

You will find throughout this book that I will share some real-life stories that might not be business related, but instead are simply about people. I find these stories inspiring, and I believe they can teach leaders how to reach the heart of the twenty-first-century culture. One thing I ask is that as you read, you allow yourself to enjoy, relax, and contemplate the questions. What you are about to receive from this book is designed to add fulfillment to your life, but be patient, it might not show up until the last sentence.

She was in those formative years, a youth who had suddenly lost her mom. As a teenager, Sue was struggling and didn't have much to hold on to. She delved into soccer as a way to keep grounded, vent her anger, and find purpose. That's when Wayne stepped in. Wayne owned successful soccer camps throughout the state of Michigan and hired Sue to coach in his summer program. The way my dear friend Sue tells it, Wayne wasn't simply a good boss he was a true mentor who took time to instruct her on the variety of strategies to think through, guide her through the coaching process, and inspire her. He also made sure Sue knew her value to the organization when he pulled her aside a couple of different times and said, "you really are great at what you do."

"That's all it took," Sue recalls. "There wasn't much of anything I wouldn't want to do for him after knowing his belief in me."

It has been thirty years since Wayne made that comment, and Sue hasn't forgotten the honest, enthusiastic assessment from one of her first bosses. When Wayne told her she was an intelligent coach, she took his word as truth because she respected him. He had taken an interest in her and given her the confidence she needed to succeed. Sue has gone on to enjoy a fulfilling career as a NCAA soccer coach who works to earn the respect of her own players. She takes time to affirm them and instill the kind of confidence that can only come from the encouraging word of a trusted leader.

    This is a story to introduce the life-changing impact one can have on another. To better understand the benefits of putting yourself in a Position of Opportunity, let's look at the flip side. Think about a time in your life when it felt like work to get up and go to your job. Maybe there was no chemistry among coworkers. Maybe your contributions were shot down in favor of keeping the status quo. Maybe you just didn't feel listened to or respected. Unfortunately, this is a far too common scenario in the modern workplace. I've talked with many individuals who feel uninspired, disrespected, and just burned out in their jobs. People who feel this way lack purpose and often see themselves as cogs in a wheel, their only value coming from performance and results. When the work culture is filled with disengaged employees just getting by, it's not hard to imagine that productivity will slip. The good news is you, as the leader, have the ability to change this. In fact, you must change this in order to catch up with the rapid changes of today's culture.

It starts with appreciating that you are significant. This in and of itself is separate from having to prove yourself and isn't due to your position of power. So many people who are hurting think power will remedy past pain. These people end up pursuing positions of leadership that they then use for self-promotion, often hurting those around them. Rather, the position of leadership is to enhance others' strengths, being at peace with who you are in or out of your work role. Resolving this aspect of ego doesn't include putting others down. In fact, a true sign of someone who possesses this personal value is being able to appreciate others' uniqueness. Having a steady, calm awareness of your own strengths and weaknesses—or another way of saying it is your light and darkness—and knowing that neither of these can take away your personhood, gives you the confidence and poise to use your position of authority as a facilitator, not a dictator.

One of the more revealing ways to see the character of a leader is how they treat others when no one is looking. We're prone to thinking that we are mostly in the light and our employees are mostly in the dark. Attempting to understand the humanness in all keeps us from viewing others as a product or profit delivery system. The inability to accept that you have just as much dark as light in you will make it more difficult to make decisions for the wellbeing of all. The sooner we admit that light and darkness are part of everyone on the planet, the sooner we will be able to live graciously and generously, and be more capable leaders in the twenty-first century.

Bill, a dear family friend, had his fair share of overbearing bosses in his younger years—those disrespectful types who valued him for his output rather than his personhood. These leaders from his past greatly influenced Bill's own leadership style when it was his turn to wear the boss hat as owner of a successful photo-printing store in St. Paul, Minnesota. Bill and his wife, Roseanna, went above and beyond for their employees, treating them with kindness and respect, offering bonuses whenever they could. They recognized their own significance in life, which gave them eyes to, in turn, appreciate the value of each employee. Bill passed away at age seventy-seven after running his shop for thirty-eight years. Roseanna shared with me how amazed she was when nearly every former employee attended Bill's funeral and shared words of appreciation and respect about their former boss.

Wayne, Bill, and many more of the leaders I've had the privilege to watch and know intuitively what Gallup researchers found in their study of the economics of wellbeing in organizations: The world's best managers see the growth of each employee as an end in itself, instead of a means to an end. When leaders see their employees as people, each with something unique and valuable to contribute to their organizations, employees begin seeing their work—and their lives—as meaningful (Rath and Harter 2010, 133)[2]. We can no longer expect people to give endless hours of unfulfilling time to a company that doesn't recognize their being as equal to what they do.

This overall sense of incorporating one's personhood directly translates into positive outcomes on the job, according to these Gallup researchers studying *Increasing Wellbeing in Organizations: The Role of Managers and Leaders*, they found employees who experienced caring managers were more likely to be top performers and produce higher quality work. They were also less likely to be sick, less likely to change jobs, and less likely to get injured on the job (Rath and Harter 2010, 135)[2].

He was a young attorney who was hired as an associate in a Denver law firm. John (anonymous name) was a bit nervous that he would mess up with his new job. When I met him, twelve years later, I asked about his favorite job and why. John looked back to that first firm.

KAI-ZEN

"Every Friday at 4 p.m., my boss would gather all of us in the office to go in the lounge. Everyone would grab a drink from the refrigerator and talk real life with each other." It wasn't a meeting or a roundup of the week's work. Instead, John remembers, "We talked about life outside the office. It didn't even matter if they were high on the seniority list or low on the ladder like me, we all gathered to talk face to face. ... I loved that!"

John also remembers that the head boss would take time to have lunch with everyone in the firm a couple times a year, just to see how they were doing. John learned a life-impacting lesson about the value of being a caring leader. He is currently treating those associates in his own law firm with a similar understanding. He sees his importance and wants to pass that importance on to others.

As leaders, you have an amazing Position of Opportunity to breathe life into your employees and watch them blossom. The full circle of this participation brings you energy as you gift them with your time and belief.

Another example of a confident and caring leader is Southwest Airlines CEO, Herb Kelleher, not only did he help develop the organizational practices that strengthen relationships, but his personal actions have exemplified the importance of relationships, starting with his employees. One of Kelleher's pilots, quoted in Jody Hoffer Gittell's book, *The Southwest Airlines Way*, made this very point: "He listens to everybody," he said. "He's unbelievable when it comes to personal etiquette. If you've got a problem; he cares" (2005, 13)[3].

Even today Marlo Larson, the butcher at our small town grocer, and I got into a conversation about this exact thing. Marlo is a steady kind of person who engages in generous living. He is known for doing thoughtful things for the local restaurants with their various special meat orders, bringing in elk, fresh Lake Superior herring, his own meat mixture recipes (which he was quoted in a recent book and is more appropriately called the art of charcuterie), and much more (Rice 2013, 121)[4]. He brought up in our discussion today how he had managed a couple of stores at one time, and how he didn't want his employees to have to put up with a sore kind of a boss. It is a conscious decision that he still makes daily, determining to enjoy at least one thing each day in order to create a healthy, lighthearted atmosphere for his employees. Marlo understands that his actions as a boss make a difference in the lives of his workers. "It's kind of important to me to lead by example," he said in his unpresuming way.

On any given day when I am by the meat counter, that is exactly what I see. He enjoys the day and enjoys the people, always asking them how they are doing. His assistants, too, carry on their duties with diligence and ease.

So, what kind of leader are you? Do you see yourself in the examples and actions of Wayne, Sue, Herb Kelleher, or Marlo? If so, I believe you're on the right track. If, though, you identify more with the disrespectful taskmasters of Bill's past, it may be time to make a change. Being an overbearing boss is not only out of fashion in today's leadership world, it's downright harmful to you, your employees, your organization, and your bottom line. Don't lose your opportunity to be the type of leader who leaves a legacy of caring, compassion, and respect. If you see value in your employees beyond what they can do for you, I invite you to embrace this Position of Opportunity and move forward with purpose. You get to be an influencer—a life changer—but the benefits come full circle as your newly engaged and empowered staff gives back to you with their energy, time, support, creativity, and commitment.

POSITION OF OPPORTUNITY

((QUESTIONS TO CONSIDER))

1. Are you still trying to prove that you are significantly valuable to yourself and to the world?

2. If you haven't already embraced the truth that you *are* important and that no one can add to or take this away from you, maybe you need to dig deeper to get these issues resolved. Would you be willing to go there and allow yourself to heal?

3. What are your strengths, the parts that are your light? How do you use this light to illuminate others?

4. In what areas in your life do you assume you have more light than others?

5. Is energy being depleted in an area, that is, your dark area?

6. In what areas of your business do you need life breathed into you?

7. In light of this chapter what kind of leader are you?

8. How can you change to be a transparent leader who mentors and guides the talented people around you?

9. How can you use your Position of Opportunity to breathe life into your people?

((CHAPTER TWO))
RELATIONAL INFLUENCES

Too often, in business and in life, we try to prove that we can make it without others. We delude ourselves into thinking that caring too much for other people might take the edge off our leadership or a bite out of productivity. I would like to offer that Relational Influences not only breathe life into you, the owner, founder, director, lieutenant, doctor, coach, teacher, manager, etc., but that they will also breathe life and give purposeful inspiration to those in your charge. Leadership for the twenty-first century needs to embrace this extraordinary relational trust factor that has the ability to connect to the core of every human being's fulfillment.

History has a way of teaching us what works in life and what doesn't. Ancient Greeks demonstrated a wise way of fostering a civilized society: communal meals. Sharing ideas across the table was part of the joy and companionship of this daily practice. All participated in the respect for the life that each one led giving them the opportunity to learn from other perspectives. What a simple, but amazing, example of Relational Influence. We can learn a lot from this civilization that persisted for 1,000-plus years and brought the world remarkable innovation and productivity. Plutarch, a Greek historian is quoted as saying, "We do not sit at the table to eat, but to eat together."[1]

Sometimes we imagine that our society is made up of autonomous individuals all looking out for number one. While there are examples of this behavior, there is no denying that, at our core, we are relational beings. Bobby Kennedy noted as much in his March 1968 address at the University of Kansas:

> We seem to have surrendered community excellence and community values in the mere accumulation of material things. ...Yet the domestic product does not allow for the health of our children, the quality of their education, or the joy of their play. It does not include the beauty of our poetry or the strength of our marriages; the intelligence of our public debate or the integrity of our public officials. It measures neither wit nor courage; neither our wisdom nor our learning; neither our compassion nor our devotion to our country; it measures everything, in short, except that which makes life worthwhile.

What is it that makes life worthwhile? The answer may be different for each of us, but I posit that, as it relates to you and your organization, the broad umbrella of relationship covers a vast majority of what most of us hold dear. The quest for what precisely this means will keep you energized and motivated to work. It will keep you focused on elevating those under your responsibility, and keep you human enough to treat others, as you would have them treat you. I would like to suggest taking this old adage a step further, to trust others, as you would want them to trust you. As a leader, you have the ability to enhance and strongly influence the relationships within your company, but you don't need to be perfect in application. Transparency builds trust and allows forgiveness when your efforts fall short. It can be overwhelming to be aware of the power that an individual has to empower another. Relational Influence is real, but it requires trust.

Roger Dow, a vice president of general sales for the Marriott Lodging Company, and Sue Cook co-authored the book *Turned On: Eight Vital Insights to Energize Your People, Customers, and Profits*. In it, they summarized this core element of trust when they wrote, "The true face of long term vitality might surprise you—the future of business lies in the ability to use modern capabilities to recapture the personal relationships of times past" (Dow, Napolitano, Pusateri, 1997, 182)[2].

This relational energy is not only for boss-employee interactions, but also for clients and partnerships within organizations that interrelate. I appreciated Dow's insight in the following statement: "My greatest fear is that too many organizations will continue to give lip service and not make building trust an uncompromising integral part of their business strategy. When we asked the people involved in the compelling case studies if they could have achieved similar results without firmly establishing trust between all parties, the answer was resounding, 'Absolutely Not!'" (Dow, Napolitano, Pusateri, 1997,182)[2].

Relational Influences happen all across the globe from military units to classrooms, from conference rooms to locker rooms. It is the substance that fills purpose in real life encounters being assured that we don't have to figure out life by ourselves. Nor do we withhold that which could help another get through her journey.

A recent study dealing with this core reflection of Relational Influence evaluates how narcissism and toxic leaders have affected the U.S. Army in "devastating the espirit de corps, discipline, initiative, drive, and willing service of subordinates and the units they comprise" (Doty & Fenlason 2013, 55-60)[3]. It was also introduced as a factor in the recent rise of suicides among Army personnel. In his January 6, 2014, report for *NPR*, "Army Takes on its Own Toxic Leadership,"[4] Daniel Zwerdling explores the study, and how toxic leadership had and is having an effect on individual soldiers and whole units. Zwerdling reports that one of the researchers, Dave Matsuda, submitted a report stating that, "(S)uicidal behavior can be triggered by... toxic command climate." This led to retired Col. George Reed, who was director of command and leadership studies at the War College, to write an article about toxic leadership in the *Military Review* (Reed, 2004, 67-71)[5]. He recalls how he was flooded with emails from soldiers who encountered toxic leaders, and how these leaders were also good at snowing their superiors—so they kept getting promoted. Reed, who now teaches leadership studies at the University of San Diego, says, "It was distressing because the Army is a world-class organization and at some point you have to ask, no, really? Are we tolerating this kind of leadership behavior?'"

In 2012, the Army revised its leadership manual, *Army Doctrine Publication 6-22*,[6] to define what toxic leadership means for the first time. The manual now states:

> "Toxic leadership is a combination of self-centered attitudes, motivations, and behaviors that have adverse effects on subordinates, the organization, and mission performance. This leader lacks concern for others and the climate of the organization, which leads to short- and long-term negative effects. The toxic leader

operates with an inflated sense of self-worth and from acute self-interest. Toxic leaders consistently use dysfunctional behaviors to deceive, intimidate, coerce, or unfairly punish others to get what they want for themselves. The negative leader completes short-term requirements by operating at the bottom of the continuum of commitment, where followers respond to the positional power of their leader to fulfill requests. This may achieve results in the short term but ignores the other leader competency categories of leads and develops. Prolonged use of negative leadership to influence followers undermines the followers' will, initiative, and potential and destroys unit morale." (Army Leadership, 2012)

Wow, that in and of itself could be expounded upon, but it is important to quote this full-length definition to understand the significance of leadership's Relational Influence. As we unfold these underlying issues at some point you have to ask, no, really? Are we tolerating this kind of leadership behavior in civilized cultures around the globe? To the Army's credit, these various reports have led to a pilot program that is currently undergoing further investigation.

As stated earlier, Relational Influence happens all across the world from military units to

RELATIONAL INFLUENCES

classrooms, to conference rooms, to doctor's offices, to locker rooms, to film sets. Having kind and respectful interactions within the walls of your organization matters. In his book *Good to Great: Why Some Companies Make the Leap and Others Don't*, Jim Collins discovered great companies were distinguished by collegial relationships that would often last a lifetime. "The people we interviewed from the good to great companies clearly loved what they did largely because they loved who they did it with" (2001, 145)[7]. As Collins found, good relationships on the job can make for a happier, more satisfied group of employees. Healthy in-office relationships can also breathe life into a business. In short, when people feel a sense of wellbeing they do better, more meaningful work. It's time to embrace this twenty-first-century style of leadership that builds trusting and influential relationships.

 The more I heard her talk, the more Barrett radiated kindness in the way she described her company's employees. She told me how she and her husband, Tom, would go out of their way to treat them with respect and appreciation. Then it dawned on me, it was *their* trash and recycling company that I was so impressed with when we moved to Denver back in 1999. It was *their* company that I loved and would tell my friends back in Michigan about. It was *their* employees who brought up our trash bins to the garage, who kindly knocked on our door if we forgot to take the trash/recycling out in time, and who had really recycled when it wasn't common at the time. Needless to say, at that point, I was certain that I wanted to meet Barrett for lunch and hear her story.

Once again this wonderful, cheerful, full of life lady was in my presence. "Well it's not much, but sure, I'll share my story," she started. I learned during that lunch that Barrett and Tom were experts at relationships, and it didn't stop with their clients. They treated their employees like family. "We always made a point to thank them several times a week for the hard work they were doing and then made sure we would get to know their families," says Barrett. "I remember there were a couple of our workers who were immigrants, really trying to get their U.S. citizenship completed over a couple of years and when it finally happened we threw a big party with the whole company to help celebrate for each of them. We certainly have had some great times together."

Then, her face dropped, "It was so hard when we sold the company, I had such a hard time saying goodbye, and leaving my helpers in the office. That was the worst part of the whole move for me. ... I so enjoyed working with them and sharing life together."

Barrett and Tom now own a moving company in

RELATIONAL INFLUENCES

the Denver area, and once again, they put staff relationships at the forefront of their business model. For some companies, the idea of treating staff like family is a good idea in theory, but it falls flat in practice. This was certainly not the case for Barrett and Tom, a point driven home in the midst of something unthinkable. Little did any of us know that four months after Barrett and I had met for lunch, a terrible tragedy would alter life for them—the loss of their twenty-two year-old in an automobile accident. I hesitate to share such a personal part of her story, and have asked permission before even including this, but she painted for me a picture that so vividly represents the results of a life lived by the Kai-Zen philosophy that made such a monumental impact on my life journey, and I believe will truly help many get the big picture.

    We actually were supposed to meet for lunch again when Barrett contacted me the day before to cancel our meeting due to her son's death. My heart dropped and I was in shock, but wanting to help in some capacity, two days later, I swung by their house to drop off some deli sandwiches to help feed whatever family was coming into town. Pulling up to the driveway, I came over a hill and was clearly able to find her house because it had eighteen to twenty cars and trucks in front. Now thinking my meager box of sandwiches wasn't going to even scratch the surface, I parked and walked to the house. Tom opened the door and warmly welcomed me. What I saw next is the picture I want to paint for the world to see.

It wasn't Thanksgiving or Christmas, but the home had that sense of warmth and closeness felt by everyone who entered. It wasn't a party, but I heard the buzz of talking in every room, even bursts of laughter at times. Of course there were tears as their son's friends, brother, and sister had gathered in the dining room to clip pictures for a memorial collage. They hugged each other as certain photos sparked different memories. I walked into the kitchen and saw Barrett surrounded by current and old employees, friends, and family, some sitting, some standing, food everywhere. And as she turned to me, in Barrett fashion, she stopped her conversation and walked over to hug and greet me with her amazing smile amidst this horrendous storm. It was absolutely a moment I shall never forget. The essence of Barrett and Tom's business is how they embrace the Position of Opportunity to breathe life back into their employees with deep respect and gratitude for the relationships, which in its wholeness lifts their being. This doesn't only apply in times of crisis, but re-energizes leaders to passionately step into the work day knowing that it's so important to embrace relational inspiration.

This, my friend, is what building trust and life

RELATIONAL INFLUENCES

into your company/organization is about! How many of you know that if something tragic happened to you, your employees/volunteers would actually be there for you? You previously breathed life into them only to know that if and when the tides change for you, they will be highly motivated to breathe life back into you.

The essence of Barrett and Tom's business is the deep respect and gratitude they have—and express—for the work their employees do, and more importantly, the people they are. Because Barrett and Tom intentionally nurture relationships within their company, employees feel energized, purposeful, and passionate. When they clock in at the start of each day, they have confidence that what they do is meaningful, valuable, and important to somebody. It's so much bigger than work, it's life.

You might be thinking, "I don't have time to incorporate this concept." You are exactly right, that is, if it isn't a priority to you. The answer may not be easy, but it is simple: You make time for what is important to you. You also make time for those things that yield success. In the Kai-Zen philosophy of success—achieving harmony, sustainable life, and innovation for you and your company—there is nothing more important than caring for the relationships that make up your industry. In my experience, the money and teamwork will follow as an organic outflow of those relationships.

Southwest Airlines gets this. The company has long been lauded for going against the grain of the typical business culture, bucking the notion that employees are simply pieces of a machine, grinding out product. In her book, *The Southwest Airlines Way,* Jody Hoffer Gittell (2005)[8] observed how Southwest's employees have been allowed to be more authentic, and self-motivated, instead of being afraid of failure. Southwest's CEO Herb Kelleher once explained, "We try to allow our people to be themselves and not have to surrender their personality when they arrive at Southwest" (Gittell, 2005, 116)[8]. An assistant station manager at the company echoed his boss' thought, and spoke on the natural result of this style of management when he said, "Employees are able to be their own [people]. This stimulates hard work and loyalty. It really seems to build loyalty. People just don't quit here. People who do leave will go to other departments" (Gittell, 2005, 117)[9]. Making this a priority has shown that employees are identifying strongly with Southwest Airlines and talking about the organization as though it were an extension of their own families (Gittell, 2005, 119)[10]. Kelleher has created a culture of relationships at Southwest where employees feel a sense of camaraderie with each other and with those in positions of leadership. This genuineness is the lubricant of a person's life song. Not only does this company want employees to find their songs, they want to hear them sing with robust enthusiasm.

Clearly, building relationships is important to creating a Kai-Zen environment on the job. But, that's just the first part. Leaders must also be open to allowing and, when appropriate, helping their employees foster positive relationships outside the workplace. Today's employees want more than fulfillment at work, they want their leaders to support fulfillment in life—from flexible schedules that allow them to spend time with their families to more freedom and autonomy to explore outside hobbies and passions. The current employees, especially the younger generation, want their lives to mean something more than the hollowness of past company protocol. Bersin highlights this in his *Forbes.com* article, writing, "'Best places to work' companies don't just have ping pong tables and free lunch, they have a 'soul,' which makes work exciting and energizing. They invest in great management and leadership. They train and develop people so they can grow. And they define their business in a way that brings meaning and purpose to the organization."[11]

Unsurprisingly, Southwest Airlines leadership gets this concept too. During research for her book, Hoffer Gittell discovered one of the keys to Southwest's success is how leaders synergize relationships in and out of the office. "The energy and learning that employees gain from building strong family and community ties can be brought into the workplace and leveraged to achieve stronger working relationships and better organizational performance. Organizations should therefore be vigilant to ensure that relationships at work do not overwhelm and undermine the family and community relationships that are needed to sustain strong working relationships" (Gittell, 2005, 123)[12].

As I walked into the coffee shop, an older gentleman with an infectious smile and warm handshake greeted me. He kindly took my offer to meet after only talking once before with him. I could tell there were a lot of stories Gary had experienced in his lifetime, and I wasn't going to let him get away without listening his nuggets of wisdom. Although he himself held some prominent positions, and helped pioneer the establishment of a south Denver community, he never gave the impression that our meeting was a waste of time. Long before Southwest was leading the way in Relational Influence, Gary told me about a manager that went that extra step to make him feel special. "It was one of my first jobs where I worked at a bank," he recalled. "I was a young guy having a lot to learn with not much experience. But my manager would always find time to sit right next to me every once in awhile and ask how I was doing, how things were at home, and if there were any business tools or resources that he could bring over to help me with my job. That really made a difference in how I went about my work there and how I managed people in future jobs."

Then Gary turned to me and emphasized, "Just keep that in mind, people won't share what they are really feeling in a conference room, you've got to spend time one-on-one in order to get to know them and find out what is important to them."

Gary has carried over these lessons in relationship building and continues in his retirement years to stay involved with friends and family and assist them with his financial resources.

We began this chapter learning from an ancient civilization, and now end it with an ancient Indian Sanskrit word, *Kula*. The word builds off this idea of having a group of diverse people outside the immediate family on whom you can rely for a sense of connection. There is a reciprocation of giving and receiving each other's best efforts that benefit all in the group. It could be when the trash talk in someone's head starts to pull them down and takes them out of their element, someone within this community of *Kula* comes alongside and believes in them more than they could believe in themselves, bringing them back into alignment with their true voice inside. There are many opportunities in an organization to help someone who is forgetting his or her greatness and could use a word of encouragement along the way. This is where the twenty-first-century leader shines their light to illuminate people's strengths and creates a type of *Kula* within the walls of their organization, admonishing growth and expansion of the people's purpose.

In her book, *A Return to Love: Reflections on the Principles of a Course in Miracles*, Marianne Williamson (1996,190)[13] wrote the following:

> "Our deepest fear is not that we are inadequate. Our deepest fear is that we are powerful beyond measure. It is our light, not our darkness that most frightens us. We ask ourselves, who am I to be brilliant, gorgeous, talented, fabulous? Actually, who are you *not* to be? You are a child of God. Your playing small does not serve the world. There is nothing enlightened about shrinking so that other people won't feel insecure around you. We are all meant to shine, as children do. We were born to make manifest the glory of God that is within us. It's not just in some of us; it's in everyone. And as we let our own light shine, we unconsciously give other people permission to do the same. As we are liberated from our own fear, our presence automatically liberates others."

RELATIONAL INFLUENCES

There just is no way to get around the idea that we are relational beings. Part of the dilemma in which we find ourselves in this shifting culture is we try to prove that we can do it without others, or that caring for people might bring too much transparency as a leader or take the edge off our business's productivity, non-profit influence or military power. That might hold some weight for the short-term, but the long-term effects increase trust and morale that will then unwrap the Relational Influences of life that hold the extraordinary keys to keeping any group of people energized and engaged. This eventually will far exceed the expectations of productivity and capture the essence of what will breathe life back into you, the leader, and achieve deep success for all.

KAI-ZEN

((QUESTIONS TO CONSIDER))

1. Are there any toxic aspects to your leadership style?

2. Are you willing to get feedback to help you improve your leadership?

3. Who in your organization do you think would come alongside you if something tragic happened later in your life?

4. How can fostering meaningful relationships with your employees, clients, army units or volunteers lead to a stronger overall workplace environment?

5. What steps can you as a leader take to develop lasting, meaningful relationships, and foster those types of relationships between coworkers in *Kula*-like fashion?

6. What can you do to promote people's trust in your own behaviors and for the whole company?

7. Can you picture how trust will not only breathe life into your company but also into your life as the leader?

((CHAPTER THREE))
THE CULTURE OF COMMUNITY

THROUGHOUT THIS BOOK, we've been looking at stories that highlight good leaders and great relationships because I believe one of the best ways to learn is from the examples of others. I've chosen to share real stories about everyone from top CEOs to the butcher in my small hometown. These leaders won't be found touting their agendas, but are more aware of those around them in generating a Culture of Community. In other words, these leaders help facilitate others to grow with a sense of dedication and trust, and the confidence to overcome the obstacles presented; to taste a fulfillment that goes beyond individual or functional tactics where the ultimate achievement is teamwork—or community—in and of itself.

In his book, *Grow to Greatness: Smart Growth for Entrepreneurial Businesses*, Edward Hess (2012, 211)[1] notes, "Culture is the glue that binds people together and to the business." That's true when the culture is good. But, if your company culture is damaged by lack of trust, or if employees perceive they are being used rather than relied upon, your culture could drive good people away. That's how important culture is. Learning to embrace and foster this all-important Culture of Community within your organization is key to creating an engaged and motivated workforce, filled with employees who not only find personal fulfillment on the job, but also work toward the betterment of the whole.

To illustrate this, let me tell you another story. I've had the opportunity to sit down with leaders of nearly every stripe throughout my life, but it's my better half, Brad, who has taught me the most about building a Culture of Community. "The industry thinks they can build successful teams by putting pieces and parts together, almost like building a type of Frankenstein ... but that won't win you a national championship," he said. And he should know. Brad played on Penn State's national championship football team in 1982, and went on to become the strength and conditioning coach for the University of Michigan's 1989 men's basketball national championship team. He was then asked by University of Michigan football legend, Bo Schembechler, in 1990 to come with him and help coach the Detroit Tigers with baseball hall of fame team manager, Sparky Anderson. He moved to the Colorado Rockies baseball team in 2000, and was given the opportunity to be a part of the process that helped build team chemistry for the 2007 team that made it to the World Series. Three different sports in three different regions of the United States, but all exhibiting the same successful team dynamic of community, trust, and respect.

THE CULTURE OF COMMUNITY

Brad wouldn't be one to let you know of this extensive background, but he was willing to share them in print if only to benefit as many sectors of life as possible. "The respect, friendship, and trust that was developed happened when many of the players on that Rockies team were in the rookie leagues. The time [spent] developing relationships when they were at the lower ranks, where they had to overcome the hardships that being in the rookie league entails, carried over that bond of community to the Big League clubhouse. The 2007 team didn't have that one player who would make or break the team's success. It was those who weren't even in the line-up who held a valuable position with the team's dynamic. They sincerely enjoyed each other on and off the yard, knowing that they had each other's backs. They all knew and accepted that it took a team."

In their book, *The Wisdom of Teams*, Jon R. Katzenbach and Douglas K. Smith (1993, 38)[2] commented on how Burlington Northern strategized with the business culture of teams to complete a very large task, which actually succeeded beyond their expectations due to the group effort. It was observed that the teams "developed a concern and commitment for one another as deep as their dedication to the vision they were trying to accomplish. They looked out for each other's welfare, supported each other whenever and however needed, and constantly worked with each other to get done whatever had to get done. Furthermore, they genuinely enjoyed each other's company. Spokesperson for one of the teams, Bill Greenwood, said, 'It was always fun inside the team. You could really let your guard down. We always really liked being around each other'" (Katzenbach and Smith 1993, 38)[2].

Brad's own experience was similar to that of the Burlington Northern team. He recalls the reward in seeing that instrumental commitment to each other for the success of the whole. "It's knowing that there has been a bond formed that, when apart, is still an element that will always be in them so that when they see each other several years later, the same element is there as if time never passed". This chemistry of relational community is part of his passion and fulfillment as a coach, guiding players to see that their purpose is bigger than just themselves and baseball. The reward is the bond of trust in and of itself that will never fade away.

Whether in athletics or military, non-profits or business, those who fail to take relationships and community into account are missing the boat. When leaders get too focused on themselves and their immediate needs or even on individual team members, they're almost guaranteed to end up forcing interaction of the pieces and parts that lead to a type of Frankenstein's monster rather than mature individuals who choose to enter into the community or team bond.

So, how do you cultivate a Culture of Community in which employees are engaged, motivated, and driven to succeed? Before we walk through specific action steps, it's important to take a hard look at yourself and dig a bit deeper. Creating a Culture of Community has to start with a seismic shift in your thinking. I've identified three questions to ask yourself in order to determine whether you're ready to start down the road toward becoming a healthier leader in order to promote a company culture of trust. I hope when you get to the end of this list, you'll find yourself answering all three questions with an emphatic *yes,* and champing at the bit to get started.

DO YOU BELIEVE IN THE BIGGER PICTURE?

Cultivating a Culture of Community within your organization is not always going to be easy. There are times when it won't feel worth it. But, over time you will see small indicators of success that will build your confidence. One of the most important decisions you can make as a business leader is to keep your focus on the big picture. Your business decisions now will not only affect you and your current employees, they could influence generations to come. Without the belief that this process is worth the effort and the resolve to stay the course, you're almost guaranteed to buckle under the first crisis situation that arises and revert to a more comfortable way of operating. Creating a Culture of Community isn't something that produces bottom-line success overnight. It takes time for you and your employees to trust one another and build lasting relationships—especially if your past leadership style was focused more on profits than people.

Tom A. Muccio, vice president of customer business development for Proctor and Gamble Worldwide, gave a presentation at the first leadership symposium sponsored by NAMA in the fall of 1996 emphasizing, Organization to Organization Trust. I believe we can learn from his definition within the walls of our unit, company, or team. In his address, Muccio described the way you build trust, "is by making yourself vulnerable, and the way the other party responds to not take advantage of you in that vulnerable position confirms the trust and allows it to build to the next level" (Dow, Napolitano & Pusateri 1998,106)[3]. Later, he lists the biggest detriment to building that trust, "Staffing people who are inflexible and too internally focused set the trust levels back at a rate that was two to three times faster than it had taken to build" (Dow, Napolitano & Pusateri 1998,110)[4]. As Muccio summarized his various experiences in

THE CULTURE OF COMMUNITY

this influential position, he wisely stated, "Establishing trust between companies is not easy, is often fragile, and requires significant maintenance to sustain. However, having lived the benefits for the last ten years, I can't believe there's any better way to do business" (Dow, Napolitano & Pusateri 1998,113)[5]. People will carry these same beliefs whether they are your clients, your staff, your class, your unit, or your team. It is best for us to pay attention to our responses and keep their trust as leaders.

ARE YOU IN IT FOR THE RIGHT REASONS?

Businesses love to craft mission statements and vision paragraphs that tout a caring company with employees who feel like family. Your employees are smart people—that's why you hired them! They also are going to sense very quickly whether your claims of family and community are genuine or just words on a wall. Do you have the heart and patience to stick this concept through? Remember, that as you give of yourself in this capacity, you, as the leader, will begin to have a bounce in your step that will reignite your energy and zeal for life. But, if you decide to buckle and retreat at this point, it will reveal that you are only using it as a tool or technique to control them, rather than encouraging their growth.

KAI-ZEN

The easiest way for me to illustrate this is to dive back into sports. Front office personnel often try to create a quick Culture of Community by piecing together a team full of players who have stellar stats and proven performance, regardless of their character and relational competence. Creating a Frankenstein-style team full of great players who lack the ability to work and play well with others is nearly always a recipe for disaster. Sure, this team will most likely come on strong in the first half of the season, but success quickly wanes where post-season possibilities of play are slight. These teams usually aren't able to keep their performance at a consistent level because management was more focused on finding a star than creating a team, and each player is consequently focused on himself rather than the whole. Not only can this be a distraction, athletes and employees can get desensitized to the management's claim of family only to be yelled at and traded once they get into a slump.

The same holds true in business. If you constantly tout the ideas of *family* and *community*, yet your employees see you looking out for number one—whether that's giving undeserved preferential treatment to a few favorites, hoarding the business' spoils rather than responding in gratitude to those who support you, or overreacting and firing people without giving them a chance to be taught—your

THE CULTURE OF COMMUNITY

words will ring hollow. This kind of hypocritical behavior can result in negative energy that will sap the life out of you, the leader, and your company culture.

CAN YOU STEP UP THEN LET GO?

You're the leader, and as you know, that means you're often the one who needs to take control and get things done. If not you, then who? Creating a Culture of Community actually takes the edge off of this belief and requires dedication, humility, and the willingness to stick with the process. Being a leader means a willingness to loosen the reigns of control and listen to feedback and suggestions from employees. Are you willing to step up and do the hard work involved? Are you willing to take blame when something goes wrong instead of assigning it to others? Are you then willing to listen to your people and truly absorb their suggestions and concerns? This becomes that inner choice to truly signal to your company that you are all in.

Author and University of Michigan business professor, Jane Dutton, puts it this way: "If leaders can be vulnerable and open, employees feel safer and more motivated to reciprocate." To match this belief, she gives the example of a prominent leader in DuPont, Dick Knowles, who stepped into a messy situation yet, over the years both he and the plant he managed became reputable. Knowles was controlling at first, but then admitted there were better ways to handle the position. This led him to take the leap of leadership and speak to his team. Dutton recounts what he said in her book *Energize Your Workplace: How to Create and Sustain High-Quality Connections at Work*, "'Maybe what I'm doing is disenabling you folks. Would you be willing to talk to me about that?' All but one of them spent about an hour telling me how great it was when I wasn't there, and what a jerk I was. They said I'd jump on them, wouldn't let them finish sentences, that I'd be really hard on someone if I thought they had done something wrong. It wasn't fun to have to sit there and listen to all this stuff, I can tell you. There was a lot of pain in me, and I cried a bit after that" (Dutton, 2003, 162-163)[6].

You might think that adapting this philosophy will weaken you and your grip, but I want to suggest that this is where problem solving with vivacity and authentic inseparable bonding soars within you and the people in your company. It does take a good dose of humility to operate this way. How easy it is to let being the boss go to our head. It's not hard to convince ourselves that we deserve all those extra perks and benefits. After all, look how hard we've worked to get to this position. Be warned, using your power to control those under you will only

THE CULTURE OF COMMUNITY

come back to bite you in the end. Authority is the quiet but steadfast strength that invigorates the growth of others and, in turn, breathes life back into the leader and all those involved.

Building confidence in your employees' capability to overcome obstacles is fulfilling in and of itself. But the ultimate achievement that goes beyond individual or functional agendas is teamwork, collaboration and community. This is a culture where the leader knows life is good and wants others to enjoy life just as much. Dutton and her assistant, Laura Atlantis, did a marvelous job of researching the key elements that make a Culture of Community, or as they termed it, "high quality connections for organizations" (Dutton, 2003,139-145)[7]. They came up with four components that promote these values: (1) valuing teamwork, (2) valuing the development of people, (3) valuing the whole person, and (4) valuing respect and the dignity of others. When a group of people can trust and respect one another's abilities to overcome the obstacles and know that when they leave their seat to sacrifice themselves to get the task accomplished, their seat isn't taken, in fact, they are warmly received by the group who has filled in the gap to keep it clean and tidy for them to come back to. It's when we ask each other, "What can I do to help you?"

KAI-ZEN

These three queries are for leaders of all shapes and sizes to look at and contemplate in order to implement a Culture of Community in their places of influence. It is evident that it's the groundwork in every thread of life. Woven into the fabric of each story—from my personal encounters to lessons gleaned from experts at Fortune 500 companies—is an unwritten code of community. May I offer that if you choose not to learn from the successes and failures of others, if you choose not to make teamwork a priority, if you choose not to focus your attention and energy on caring for and cultivating relationships within your company, you could end up with Frankenstein's monster? You'll be cobbling together pieces and parts, struggling to make the whole operation work, when others are out there winning national championships.

THE CULTURE OF COMMUNITY

((QUESTIONS TO CONSIDER))

1. What kind of culture does your organization exude currently?

2. What are some obstacles that would need to be removed in order to implement Culture of Community–based decisions?

3. What is your motivation for improving your company culture?

4. Are you, as a leader, willing to do the hard work it takes to create a positive, healthy culture among your employees?

5. What could the payoff be for you and your company if you choose to foster a Culture of Community?

6. What will continue to drain your energy and growth as a person if you choose not to focus on building community within your organization?

7. How can you implement real discussions of transparency with your trusted managers or supervisors in order to receive fresh ideas and vital changes?

KAI-ZEN

8. Will you be able receive your employees' ideas for change, then go back to them in order to review which changes or ideas will be implemented, and finally compliment their ability to risk being truthful with you?

9. Would you then celebrate the little victories along the way and see that you are an amazing leader by choosing this philosophy?

((CHAPTER FOUR))
IMPLEMENTING SMALL STEPS TO SUCCESS

THERE WAS AN EAGERNESS on her seven-year-old face to get out on those waves as she stood at the shore, surf board in one hand her other grasping her dad's. Her expression gained more and more determination with each wave she watched. She beamed with a fresh joy about this new adventure, and walked confidently into the ocean with her dad. He wasn't expecting the first wave he chose to launch her on would grow so big. Before he could swim to her, the damage had been done. Out from the crashing wave were two little legs pointing toward the sky. She didn't cry, but as she regained her whereabouts, she climbed right out of the water and ripped that surfboard attachment band off her wrist. Her face had lost the energy and the smile.

This lesson doesn't change, as we get older. In our eagerness to learn something new, we at times take on a big wave expecting immediate success without remembering that there will need to be some adjustments. The overestimated ability to tackle such a huge leap turns in on ourselves and we end up fighting feelings of failure. Being able to break the big wave down to smaller waves will allow a firmer footing to accomplish the goal. The same is true for those you lead. Don't expect them to be able to succeed by launching them onto a big wave either. This is where it would be valuable to prepare your people with the tools they need to gain confidence and achieve competency in handling projects. In order to kindle energy and expectancy of success, you must learn how to break things down into smaller steps. It is vital for the foundations of innovation to be built solidly and prevent future decay from rapid ascension.

By the way, there is a happy ending to this little girl's story. Good 'ole dad came alongside his daughter on the beach and kneeled down to her level. He must have spoken some words of encouragement, because the next thing I knew, she put that surf board attachment back on her wrist and—though holding onto her dad's hand a little tighter this time—walked back into the waves. Even though it did take a couple more times of practice on the smaller waves to build her confidence back up, soon she was riding those waves and laughter filled the air…and she didn't want to stop doing it over and over.

My friend, it is necessary for us as leaders to know that we will make some bad calls. Those we are leading might lose confidence in our judgments, which could diminish the morale, but if we take the time to look in the mirror, to admit, listen to our hearts, and build that belief back into them, we will

IMPLEMENTING SMALL STEP TO SUCCESS

receive kindness and forgiveness, and regain their trust—and they won't want to stop.

We're talking about substantial changes here. People will forgive, but not endlessly, so choose wisely. As you are attempting to make Kai-Zen your practice, there will be bumps along the way, but you are not completely alone in this, I do believe that the divine intelligence of this universe will open doors of opportunity as you embark on adapting this exercise of including the humanizing of others in your thought process. I have found that those who solidly embrace Kai-Zen will experience an inward transformation that will lead them to a clairvoyant sense of how to break down the larger leaps into manageable tasks. You will know when you've jumped too far ahead and then need to concede there was a better way. You will grow to see how much more the group will get done as you entrust others to mature in their confidence. When you find that humble poise, having a knowledge and honest appreciation of yourself, it will bring openness to another way of thinking. Embracing the differences in others will actually give back to you a tremendous amount of energy.

In this chapter, I will lay out several small, but substantial action items to help you take the philosophy of "humanizing the workplace for the wellbeing of all" from concept to practice. This profound, personal transformation will guide you in building that all-important Culture of Community within your company. In this way, you'll be better able to lead, inspire, and nurture those around you.

STEP ONE: LISTEN

If you really think about it, listening shouldn't be that hard for us to do. It requires no special talent to listen. Yet, in our distracted, fast-paced life it gets passed by. A leader understands that listening is more important than talking in order to represent the interests of the whole group. As a leader, it is important to allow others to finish their explanations, even if it is a volatile discussion, before you speak. This allows freedom of thought and free-flowing ideas. In his book, *The Lost Art of Listening*, Dr. Michael Nichols (2009, 14)[1], a professor of Psychology at the College of William and Mary writes, "To listen is to pay attention, take an interest, care about, take to heart, validate, be moved...appreciate. Listening is so central to human existence as to often escape notice; or, rather, it appears in so many guises that it's seldom recognized as the overarching need that it is."

She did a wonderful presentation for our weekly business owner meeting in Denver. From our very first conversations over coffee before this meeting, I could tell she was a natural nurturer and well suited for her job as a therapist. In fact, Jen is one of the

IMPLEMENTING SMALL STEP TO SUCCESS

lead therapists in the Cherry Creek District of Denver. As her talk came to a close, I knew I needed to ask her just one more question. It was evident that her pure intentions would give me an answer that would be undeniably true about one of the keys to humanity. Once we were dismissed, I raced to catch up with her. We walked out to the parking lot together, and I asked her to expand on what she'd said about working with some of the worst juvenile offenders in New Mexico earlier in her career. I asked, "What was it that tipped them from a life of crime to a more positive direction?" Jen didn't hesitate, "When someone took the time to listen to them on a consistent basis, their lives started to have purpose and drive. It was when they were heard that they began to change for the better." Wow, that's it! What can breathe life into a human being? Being heard by those who care! Of course, with our teams, companies, units, organization, or classes made up of people, this must similarly motivate them also. You'd think we'd catch on by now that this simple but profound fact will help us and gift others with a more fulfilling life at home and in the workplace.

To make listening a top priority in your organization, start by meeting with your managers on a regular basis to do more than just talk business. You may spend a portion of this scheduled time going over responsibilities, but it's also critical to carve out time to simply listen, and listen well. It may take some practice to perfect the art of listening. For Nichols, "the essence of good listening is empathy, which can be achieved only by suspending our preoccupation with ourselves and entering into the experience of the other person. Part intuition and part effort, it's the stuff of human connection" (Nichols, 2009,10)[2].

To truly connect with your people, these meetings need to be about them. Allow your employees the space and freedom to talk about the hard and the good stuff that is going on at work and outside the office walls. You might even create a folder of information on each manager with whom you meet to help you remember personal details that came up during the course of your meeting. Writing down their concerns and ideas, likes and dislikes, gives you insight into what you can be doing better and ideas for how to help your employees succeed. Then, when you meet again, you can review this file and stay current with questions to follow up from the last meeting. This brings a sense of connection and assurance that they are significant. On the contrary when they don't remember, you feel more like a science experiment than a person. Putting this into practice will set an example for your team of how they can do the same with their supervisors or next level of authority within your organization.

IMPLEMENTING SMALL STEP TO SUCCESS

While this process can happen organically, if you're serious about making it a priority, sit down with your calendar and mark out possibly fifteen minutes a week for each manager. Plan monthly breakfasts and get them on the books. If you don't schedule it, other things will likely crop up and take the place of these important encounters. Have open forums to allow the ideas and constructive criticism of management to flow. Encourage transparency to build the trust needed for this extraordinary relational factor that has the ability to connect the core of every human being's fulfillment globally.

The Leader's Bank offers a great example of leaders who choose to listen. In *Grow to Greatness*, Hess (2012, 173)[3] writes about Lynch, the CEO of this high-performance community banking business, who believes that some of the best ideas come from his front-line employees and describes the communication among his staff as an "open, two-way street." Lynch explains, "Because we view our employees as being leaders themselves, we give them the authority to make decisions without always having to check with their superiors. In staff meetings, we consider all ideas good ideas."

In one example, Leader's senior vice president and director of human resources, Ritter, recalled a time when the company experienced an intense growth spurt. With all the new hires, current employees were concerned company-wide communication would break down. In typical good-culture fashion, Lynch made it a point to listen to his employees' concerns and address them. He started by adding dinners with the CEO and breakfast with the board of directors where employees could be heard and understood in a more intimate setting. The company also launched an employee newsletter to ensure the lines of communication stayed open. "We're proactive about getting folks' opinions about the strength of the organization, and then we address these things before they have a chance to take root and influence our culture," Ritter said (Hess, 2012, 175)[4].

Taking the time to truly listen to your people is a crucial part of understanding what specifically breathes life into the whole group. Knowing this gives you a glimpse into what drives your people and what gives or takes energy and a sense of wellbeing in your employees.

STEP TWO: MENTOR AND TRAIN

A mature leader is one who develops a desire to mentor another's growth, breathing belief in the other until he or she sees the ability to succeed, and in turn wants to pass that experience down to mentor and believe in someone else. This becomes a type of song that goes on and on because of the depth of commitment one receives from their leader

IMPLEMENTING SMALL STEP TO SUCCESS

is never forgotten. Taking the time to respectfully introduce new employees to the company and incorporating ongoing training to help them understand their roles, conflict resolution, and responsibilities is of paramount importance. It will bring a sense of confidence to know what is being asked of them and will give them the tools to succeed with the task at hand. If you choose not to break their assignments down into these teaching moments, you will be setting them up for failure. This is asking them to ride a huge wave as we saw in the story of the seven-year-old surfer, that will shake their determination and take their energy out from underneath them.

In her book *Energize Your Workplace,* Dutton observes: "When MBA students in my classes describe the poor job most firms do in training their interns, it reminds me that we cannot take task enabling for granted. In their case, and in the case of most people in organizations, when opportunities for training are present and not delivered on, not only is a chance to form a meaningful connection forgone, but also employees withdraw commitment and engagement for the organization. Poor task enabling can undercut employee loyalty and attachment" (2003, 58)[5].

Let me summarize. Failing to set your people up for success by implementing solid training and mentoring can lead to detached employees who lack connection to your organization and motivation to work for the betterment of the whole. That's why making the time to do this is so important. When individuals feel well prepared and equipped for success, they are far more likely to go after their work with passion and proficiency.

Trilogy Health Services' Randy Bufford reinforced this idea when he said, "If we take great care of our employees, they take great care of our customers, we have a bottom line. Our challenge as we grow is to make sure that we keep the culture high and don't lose sight of our mission" (Hess 2012, 356)[6].

One of my children is encountering her first full-time job, and due to her efforts has been promoted three levels within fifteen months. At nine months, the honeymoon phase was wearing out and the daily grind was kicking in. We began to talk about the different roles and personalities she was encountering daily. Because she was conscientious about her responsibilities, she was aware of who would slack and those who would consistently work. In the process, her role started to pick up with more supervisory tasks to the point that she was getting anxious with the load she knew was going to get piled on her each day. Several months later I began asking a few questions, where I learned from her that not only were they short staffed with managers, the manager she had was trying to slip away during the day from doing his job. As this consistently reoccurred, my husband and I tried to encourage her. In the meantime we thought to ourselves, if this company doesn't break and take care of their inner management team, our daughter should probably start looking for a company that embraces innovative change for the peaceful good of all. But to her credit, she stuck it out a few months more and was rewarded with a new manager who made a world of difference. Oh the power of one human soul. That human is you and it's me!

Because that individual actually stayed engaged with his role as manager and didn't try to slip away, because he took the time to explain points of conflict that she had encountered with clients and taught her how to respond with a better understanding, and because he cared for her growth as a person, he made a profound impact on her life. She is now looking forward to learning from him each day, and senses empowerment to handle various client relations. This ultimately is building confidence in her ability to do the job well and treat others with the same respect she is receiving from him. The probability of her wanting to replicate this in her future managerial roles is much higher due to the mentorship of one human soul to another.

Establishing a template for training and mentoring will take time and commitment. But, a solid method for teaching both new hires and those who are promoted into a new position is foundational to the quality and success of your organization. Your people will feel valued when they know you are investing time and resources into their growth as individuals. You will also attract those who want to develop their skills. There are plenty of resources online and in bookstores about how to train effectively, and I encourage you to seek out those that are relevant to your specific needs. My hope is simply to reinforce the vital need for effective and comprehensive training to help you equip your people to succeed and, in turn, sense a fulfillment that your life and theirs is meaningful.

STEP THREE: COMMUNICATE

Creating an atmosphere of open communication is an essential part of Kai-Zen. It is paramount for employees to admit mistakes without fearing they will lose their jobs. William Holland, chairman and CEO of United Dominion Industries in Charlotte, North Carolina, said, "In my opinion, there is one basic policy that tolerates no exceptions: play it straight with the public, stockholder, customers, suppliers, employees, or any other individual or group. The only right way to deal with people is forthrightly and honestly. If mistakes are made, admit them right away and correct them as soon as possible" (quoted in Dow, Napolitano and Pusateri

IMPLEMENTING SMALL STEP TO SUCCESS

1998, 175)[7]. Remember how the great inventors had to embrace mistakes in order to overcome their fear of failure? They needed to have a sense that they were entrusted to figure out a solution and not to worry about their humanness that undoubtedly would show up every once in awhile.

We've already emphasized in chapter three that a leader needs to be vulnerable in admitting his shortcomings in order to build trust. Transparent communication will promote the advancement of your employees' innovations. "A leader's willingness to be vulnerable and emotionally accessible creates a healthy basis for authentic connecting, building a foundation for high-quality relationships. ... Where these relationships happen, communication improves, problem-solving energy is released and the firm as well as the employees benefit" (Dutton 2003, 163)[8].

Something else that could be standing in the way of your communication is technology. No doubt, it has done great things for this world. But, with everyone in the workplace seemingly spending more time with devices than with people, there is a glut of technology alone time that can keep us from the all-important face-to-face interaction that is also a part of the communication factor to establish a Culture of Community and trust.

As Dr. Atul Gawande demonstrates in his book *The Checklist Manifesto: How to Get Things Right*, communicating face-to-face can and should be an important part of your business in order to avoid complications. Gawande saw the difference it made not only in his medical profession, but also in many other industries. "The assumption was that anything could go wrong, anything could get missed. That's the nature of complexity. But it was also assumed that, if you got the right people together and had them take a moment to talk things over as a team rather than as individuals, serious problems could be identified and averted" (2011, 66)[9].

Gawande also postulates if we were to entrust more minds to participate in the solution, that we would end up making less mistakes due to personal communication. "The builder trusted in the power of communication," he writes. "They didn't believe in the wisdom of the single individual, of even an experienced engineer. They believed in the wisdom of the group, the wisdom of making sure that multiple pairs of eyes were on a problem and then letting the watchers decide what to do. Man is fallible, but maybe men are less so" (67)[10].

I can hear some of you protesting: "But we're a *virtual* company with employees all over the world, surely you understand we can't meet face-to-face!" Technology has allowed for myriad business models in recent years. You may have a brick and mortar location that houses some of your employees while others telecommute. You may manage a slough of

IMPLEMENTING SMALL STEP TO SUCCESS

contractors who you've never met in person. Or, you may operate solely online, communicating via e-mail or over the phone. Whatever the arrangement, interacting face-to-face and allowing many perspectives adds a level of connectedness that is hard to match. Thankfully, technology has devised ways for colleagues around the globe to meet as if sitting in a room with one another. Video chat platforms like Skype and Google Hangout allow you to get in the same room with employees, even share a meal or a cup of coffee, and connect face-to-face. The ability to adapt to your people's situations will be a pivotal point of creating a culture of camaraderie and respect. Trilogy's president, Randall Bufford, makes real life, in person, communication a priority. "Our employees see a lot of me, and also the COO and the area managers. Occasionally I'll sub in if we have an area manager's position open. I might grab two or three facilities and just take those under my wing, because it keeps me close to the business and sharp on management and things on the field level" (Collins 2001, 235)[11]. Bufford goes on to explain, "that to build and maintain an environment that resulted in high employee engagement required a culture of constant improvement" (236)[11]. It is this ability to communicate face-to-face, frankly, and freely with multiple minds involved that will then bring about advancement and a culture of wellbeing.

KAI-ZEN

STEP FOUR: ADAPT AND FACILITATE

Part of being a savvy business leader is the willingness to understand your current circumstances and adapt to meet the needs of clients and the market at large. This is also true when it comes to successfully creating a Culture of Community for employees and volunteers. People value flexibility that allows them to pursue family obligations, hobbies, and volunteer opportunities outside of the office. Understanding the dynamics of your own industry and making wise adaptations to facilitate the feedback given, goes a long way towards building the all-important Culture of Community.

One of my client's, Sandra Coen, is the founder of the James Resource Network, an organization dedicated to providing quick access to supportive services that establish stability for transitional single parents. When she founded her nonprofit in 2007, Sandy put a lot of thought into creating a Culture of Community in her organization that would not only breathe life into her clients—primarily single mothers—but also into her employees and volunteers.

As we discussed her vision for her own organization, Sandy brought up EChO, a Christian outreach program in Evergreen, Colorado. "It really

IMPLEMENTING SMALL STEP TO SUCCESS

is quite remarkable," she told me. "They have an amazing set up where their volunteers actually stay around to help for ten to fifteen years."

I asked, "How do you think they manage to do that?"

"Well one thing that stands out is…that they have set up their volunteers to be scheduled in teams for when they come in to volunteer, it usually is at the same time slots during the week. That way they get to see the same people each block of time that they work, which is probably building that sense of connection, kind of like a second family to them. …That must be a strong factor for them wanting to stay involved with volunteer work for such a long time," she replied.

Sandy has taken EChO's example to heart and has already started to incorporate this volunteer model into her organization in an effort to reinforce the Culture of Community she envisions. She knew this model would work for her based on its success at EChO, and because she knew her volunteers would enjoy consistency in scheduling and working as part of a team. On the other hand, if you are running a business rather than a volunteer organization, it may be necessary to value flexibility in scheduling over creating a consistent group dynamic.

This was the case at Southwest Airlines when it came to scheduling flight attendants. "Some airlines have attempted to schedule the same employees to work together on particular flights over the course of an extended period, hoping to build more permanent teams. But Southwest decided against such scheduling practices, not wanting to reduce the scheduling flexibility enjoyed by Southwest employees. In effect, Southwest did not want to sacrifice the family relationships of its employees to build stronger working relationships. Southwest looks for synergies between family and work relationships and tries to avoid trading off one for the other" (Hoffer Gittell 2005, 212)[11].

In short, employees value companies that allow them to pursue family obligations, hobbies, and volunteer opportunities. Nestlé Purina Petcare Company has undertaken this concept by allowing its employees to bring their pets to work. According to the company's website,[13] there's even a dog park on site. What a simple but great way to incorporate what's important to their people. The dynamics of your own industry and making wise adaptations to facilitate feedback goes a long way toward building the all-important Culture of Community.

Another area in which companies are increasingly called upon to understand and adapt is the so-called generation gap. Often, communication between leaders and employees begins to break down at this most fundamental level, and can cause problems within a company that range from

IMPLEMENTING SMALL STEP TO SUCCESS

stymieing growth to a full-on breakdown in the corporate structure.

As a CEO, founder, lieutenant, director, coach or boss who is firmly planted in the Baby Boom generation, or even the early side of Generation X, it can be hard to put yourself in the shoes of a Millennial (by some estimations, those born after 1980). In recent years, the catchphrase YOLO has popped up on social media sites like Twitter and Facebook. It means You Only Live Once, and I believe it perfectly exemplifies the attitudes and thought processes of the generation now entering the workforce. If you were to jump into the mind of one of your 20-30 year old employees, you might hear something like this: "I only live once, and the reality is, I could die at any moment in a mall, school, movie theater, the Boston Marathon, or on an airplane at the mercy of a terrorist. So I am going to make sure my life counts now. I need to feel fulfilled and have a purpose, with work that is important and people who make life meaningful to me."

Hear this leaders: If Millennials don't sense they are making a difference in the world with their work, their hobbies, or their friends, forget them sticking around. It is important for them to bring their authentic selves to work, to know they can be relational at work and not need to put on a different face than who they really are. They will do much better if you facilitate their strengths by allowing them to participate in determining who in the group should take which role. What I mean is, in the initial process of sorting through different responsibilities for a project, you begin to give them the outcomes that are needed and share the tools that will be needed, but then let them discuss amongst the group and designate the who and the what. The act of figuring it out on their own will be more motivating for them than if they were to take direction from an authority figure. What gives them a sense of deep purpose is knowing that the group is depending on them to come through. This then is the ultimate challenge for a facilitator: to start them moving, but then get out of the way.

Having a true Culture of Community in the workplace is crucial for this relational generation in choosing their place of employment, and when it comes to keeping them there. Organizations that begin to embrace—rather than balk at—how young workers think and operate can swing open the doors to a generation of creative, motivated, and passionate employees who are looking for a cause to embrace. I believe this shift in thinking could be an integral part of the revitalization your organization. Adapting your leadership style in this twenty-first century, and understanding how to facilitate generational differences could also be a primary determiner of your company's success.

IMPLEMENTING SMALL STEP TO SUCCESS

These steps are small but substantial. Together they make up the core principles of the Kai-Zen philosophy. Choosing to move toward a Kai-Zen company through measured and intentional steps will show your employees you are committed to their growth, success, and sense of purpose both in and out of the office. As you show respect for and trust in your employees, they will naturally mirror that attitude back to you in their behavior, work ethic, and willingness to go the extra mile for your company.

Dutton sums up the importance of this type of give-and-take when she writes:

> This process of mutual trusting will strengthen our belief in each other's trustworthiness. Trust thus creates a higher-quality connection as both people in a trusting connection expect high-integrity behavior from each other. In trusting connections, both people experience more freedom to be authentic, to let their guard down and to be flexible. Less time is spent monitoring or trying to discern intentions of the other person. In a trusting connection, the default value is that you believe the other person is acting with your best interests in mind. Trust feeds learning and flexibility in a unit. (2003, 82)[14]

KAI-ZEN

We can talk about the importance of listening, training, communicating, and understanding how to flexibly facilitate, but once you see that these small but significant steps inject life, purpose, and fulfillment into your employees—and by extension your organization—failing to embrace them will only keep you in an old-school thinking pattern that will not succeed in this century. These steps are your leaping off point. Follow them to create a solid foundation on which to breathe life into your leadership and your people for many years to come.

IMPLEMENTING SMALL STEP TO SUCCESS

((QUESTIONS TO CONSIDER))

1. Are you asking anyone to take too big of a leap, thus setting him up for failure?

2. What small steps are you willing to implement today that could begin to breathe life back into your business?

3. What might the result be if you truly took time to listen to your employees?

4. Do you need to become more transparent with your communication?

5. What areas have frequent breakdowns because of the lack of communication?

6. How can you incorporate ongoing training for your faithful crews who have stayed on board?

7. How can you listen better to facilitate your people and your organizational culture?

8. In what areas do you need to bridge the generational gap?

KAI-ZEN

9. What are some ways to give younger (and all) workers flexibility?

((CHAPTER FIVE))
SUSTAINABLE ENERGY

"KNOW THYSELF," Socrates famously said. "Know your strengths and weaknesses, your relation to the universe, your potentialities, your spiritual heritage, your aims and purposes; take stock of thyself." (Kelly, 2004, 238)[1]

One of the key traits that I've observed in great leaders is the ability to look within and truly understand their own being. When you start from a place of knowledge and understanding of yourself, your past, what drives you, you are better able to stay engaged with the people, accepting both failure and success as part of the territory that comes with your position. I think if we were all to follow Socrates' advice, there would be more energized leaders out there reaching out to breathe life into their organizations. But keeping this passion afloat amid the ambush of responsibilities, as a leader, is always a challenge. This re-energizing is essential for the twenty-first-century leader to maintain effectiveness for a growing business. Blending personhood and work is what we need to wrestle with to bring about a more fulfilling life, and to pay forward what you have received.

As you look within to improve the overall wellbeing of yourself and thus your employees, there are three variables that are substantially important to sustaining your energy as a leader: understanding your being, accepting your own humanness, and finding people who are a good fit.

STATE OF WELLBEING

There are many leadership books out there that give various techniques to follow, but with all of those tools, where have you allowed yourself the time to understand your state of being? In my opinion, one of the main differences between a wise leader who stays the course and a foolish one who gets distracted and fades away, is the ability to know and appreciate himself or herself separate from his or her role at work—or, what I call the *Do* Mode. Leaders who don't know themselves in this respect tend to misuse leadership to gain power over others. In fact, my theory is that those who lead tyrannically have never been affirmed for their personhood, and haven't tasted this state of wellbeing, but are instead compelled to prove something to themselves and to the world. The ability for someone who doesn't understand and peacefully respect himself to try to exhibit this Kai-Zen philosophy towards his employees is not very likely. And yet, many participate in this misuse of position simply because they know no other way.

Just think for a moment about your best bosses. Were they the ones who were insecure and short-

SUSTAINABLE ENERGY

fused, or did they maintain a sense of calm and confidence even in the midst of chaos? If you see glimpses of yourself in the former description, or if you struggle with wanting to wield authority over your employees or rule with an iron fist, I suggest you take a look within and figure out why. In the first section of this chapter, I will be diving in to some of the deepest parts of personhood to help you know how to rejuvenate your passions to bring joy back into living.

To get started, ask yourself these questions: Do I carry around a sense of inadequacy? Is there a voice in my head constantly reminding me I'm not good enough, never will be, that I'm not doing it right? Are you quick to jump to the conclusion that others are disrespecting you when discussing their ideas instead of yours? If you answered in the affirmative, please don't feel these questions are meant as judgment. Simply acknowledging that you feel this way is a step in the right direction. Knowing yourself is a necessary part of replenishing your passion and enthusiasm. For example, if you continually allowed a robber to come into your house every day when you were gone and steal your property without trying to stop him, you wouldn't have much left in your home. The same goes for these condemning thoughts that are robbing you of the strength to sustain yourself and your occupation. Why do you allow them to continually steal life from you? Why do you allow negative past experiences to trickle down to those who work for you? This may seem like a more emotional journey than many in business care to take, but truly knowing and understanding yourself has vast consequences beyond just improved relationships. If you don't deal with these thoughts, they will blind you from seeing your own inherent value, and that of the people you lead.

Now, look back again. Who in your life first made you feel insecure? Maybe you had parents who believed you were only as good as what you could produce—good grades, goals on the field, a career that brought in the big bucks. Maybe you felt you could never please them. Chances are, they felt (or feel) that they were never really good enough either and that was passed down to you. Or maybe your parents were nothing but encouraging, but you had a coach or a teacher or a boss who never thought you could do anything right. Maybe you were unpopular in school and have spent the subsequent years striving to prove those cool kids wrong. Whatever in your past led you to believe you were not enough or that you'd never be enough will continue to haunt your daily life and responsibilities as a leader until the day you decide to deal with it. Please, don't let this ghost continue to rob you of the joys of life.

If the first step is becoming aware of your feelings of inadequacy, the second is forgiving those who made you feel that way. This doesn't mean you have to write a letter or call them on the phone. In fact, many on your list may have been (in their minds) acting in your best interest, not even aware they were hurting you. Simply acknowledge the role each person had in making you feel inadequate, accept that it happened, and let it go.

"Acceptance helps," writes self-help author Melody Beattie in *The Language of Letting Go* (1990, 270)[2]. "So does forgiveness—not the kind that invites that person to use us again, but a forgiveness that releases the other person and sets him or her free to walk a separate path, while releasing our anger and resentments. That sets us free to walk our own path."

When, consciously or unconsciously, you choose to stuff down old hurts, it is only a matter of time before they leak out and land on an innocent employee or family member in the form of an angry outburst or worse. The important work of forgiving and letting go is not only vital for your own emotional and mental health, it is paramount to the success and sustainability of your business. In her book *The Dynamic Laws of Prosperity*, Catherine Ponder notes:

KAI-ZEN

"We are all creatures of emotion and deep feeling, and our deep feelings can make us or break us financially. ... You should guard them as you would a gold mine, because your emotions are in reality the richest gold mine you will ever own. Scattered thinking, scattered emotions, scattered actions lead to a scattering of your mind power. This in turn depletes your physical energy that is essential for prosperity; it depletes your brain energy that is needed for an intelligent course of action or plan for prosperity; it saps your emotional drive that is needed to put your plans to work." (1985, 69)[3]

Do you know where you are on the spectrum of centered versus scattered? Start by asking yourself the following questions:

> Are you able to sit quietly, block out the sirens of the day, and wait for clarity of thought and emotion before embarking on a new project, or are your thoughts constantly running a mile-a-minute?
> Do you allow yourself grace amidst failure or do you react to failure with anger, blame, or self-abasement?

SUSTAINABLE ENERGY

To explain why these questions are important for you and your business, let me share with you a profound quote I read in the short narration, *Sara*, by Law of Attraction experts Esther and Jerry Hicks (2007)[4]. "Remember if you let the conditions that surround you control the way you feel, you will always be trapped. But when you are able to control the way you feel—because you control the thoughts you offer—then you're truly liberated."

This liberation is what will allow you to make decisions that are far more effective and productive than frantically reacting to each new situation. One of the greatest challenges for leaders is to pull themselves out of inner conflict and respond intentionally to each situation as it arises. As you make yourself a priority, and nurture your personhood in order to really appreciate your being, you will start to see you can celebrate life each day. Beattie expands on this in *The Language of Letting Go* when she writes, "Many of us are afraid that the work won't get done if we rest when we're tired. The work will get done; it will be done better than work that emerges from tiredness of soul and spirit. Nurtured people, who love themselves and care for themselves, are the delight of the Universe. They are well-timed, efficient, and Divinely led" (Beattie 1990, 97)[5].

These are hard areas to look at, and can cause a time of self-doubt. But once you embrace that it's far better to see your need for openness than to hide behind your mode of intelligence, which has nothing to do with your personhood, you'll be released from a false façade that never served you or others in the first place. Learning to be true to yourself will bring back your joy. This is a road you must travel that will truly breathe new life and energy into yourself and those around you.

YES, YOU ARE WONDERFULLY HUMAN

My hypothesis is that the type A personality isn't just genetic, sometimes it can be the result of early childhood conditioning. Someone who never sensed that they were enough for a variety of reasons may take great identity in the Do Mode and therefore, get much done. I've had to wrestle with this tendency myself. The inclination is for us to think these are the leaders—the movers and shakers—because of their drive to get things done. But the level of perfectionism that usually accompanies this trait can also create a cacophony of outrage when a type A leader demands his subordinates follow suit. It is important to weed out these intentions in order to understand what the main impetus is that drains you and your company of energy.

A humble leader recognizes his own humanness, and recognizes the inherent value of diversity of those he leads. May you hold on to this truth: humility is not weakness. Instead, humility is strength under pressure. There is true strength in understanding that compassion is more valuable than control, people are more important than profits, and life is more than just survival. This is what will yield effective results of abundant and generous innovation.

In his February 23, 2014 *New York Times* column, "How to Get a Job at Google," Thomas L. Friedman interviewed Google's senior vice president of people operations, Laszlo Bock. Bock discussed emergent leadership versus the traditional form of leadership. "What we care about is, when faced with a problem and you're a member of a team, do you, at the appropriate time, step in and lead? And just as critically, do you step back and stop leading, do you let someone else? Because what's critical to be an effective leader in this environment is you have to be willing to relinquish power."[6]

A traditional leader is often characterized by steamrolling over his employees and opponents to get what he wants. Whether this behavior is rooted in insecurity, past pain, or an inflated sense of self-importance, the behavior of a toxic leader makes everyone around him feel less than in order to buoy his own status. While this type of lone wolf is often lauded in the business world for his independence and willingness to run contrary to the pack, it might be more useful to look to those animals who work together to best understand our innate, human desire to connect and collaborate. In the documentary film, *I Am*, the narrator posits: "The herds of elk, the flocks of birds and the school of fish actually allow 51 percent of the group to be the decision maker in what direction they turn" (2011). The barbaric ways where the dominant called the shots is how we interpreted it until now. The truth of the matter is that the best leaders want to honor the suggestions of their people and be facilitators. In the process of honoring their voices, they will be able to release most responsibilities and delegate to those who come up with the significant ideas. There will also be a trust established in them, which in turn gives you a sense of connection and purpose as you help them grow. The camaraderie that is exchanged is part of that inseparable, person-to-person bond that has an unspoken power to move mountains—and your business. And yes, they are human and will make some mistakes, but that won't be their intent.

The Hicks continue to explain, "… as you're able to allow that pure love energy to flow, no matter what, in spite of the conditions that surround you—then you have achieved unconditional love. You are then, and only then, truly the extension of who you really are and who you have come here to be. You are then, and only then, truly fulfilling your purpose for being." (Hicks, 1995. 172,173)[7].

Again, this might seem too warm and fuzzy for you, but I exhort you to open your eyes to see that there is tremendous strength in the ability to humble yourself and treat others with the respect and dignity they deserve. You may also believe that if you show any sign of humility employees will take advantage of your kindness. Some may. More likely, though, your own openness will create a bond of trust and drive employees to do well in the eyes of their caring and committed boss.

I can't think of a more poignant example of this than the classic book-turned-musical-turned-feature film, *Les Misérables* (2012). Early in the musical, a priest offers shelter to ex-convict Jean Valjean. Valjean turns on the man's kindness and steals the monastery's valuable silver. He is apprehended and returned to face the priest. Instead of condemning Valjean, the priest shows him mercy, telling authorities he gave the silver to the criminal. The priest had every right to turn Valjean in for his crime, but he understood the value of offering mercy over judgment. Valjean went on to become Mayor and never forgot the mercy he was shown. He spent his entire life paying forward the kind gesture of a man who knew the value of grace.

As leaders, we may find ourselves in similar situations at one time or another. There are people who will take advantage of our kind-hearted position, but there are many more who will work with every fiber and passion in their being for you, motivated by the fact that you gave them a chance, and that you value and cherish them as individuals, not just numbers on a spreadsheet.

FINDING PEOPLE WHO ARE A GOOD FIT

This seems like a good time to turn our attention to the second key variable to sustaining energy within your organization: the type of people with whom you choose to surround yourself. As we discussed, there will be those who take advantage of a kind and gracious boss, which only makes the process of hiring more important. In a Kai-Zen company, hiring is about much more than finding someone who is qualified for the position at hand, it is about finding someone who will contribute energy to your organization rather than sap it away.

When my friend Cindy and her husband, Brian, owned a technology business, they came up with a creative way to find the right fit for their team. "Brian would actually narrow our employee search down to a few prospects and then invite them to do something leisurely with him, whether it be a bike ride, tennis, golf, or something where they felt relaxed. That allowed him to see who they truly were, rather than just seeing them in an interview,"

SUSTAINABLE ENERGY

Cindy shared. "We learned this after finding out the hard way, but then were so thankful how this kept us from wasting invaluable time with someone who wasn't a good fit for us."

You may not have time to golf with every candidate for every job within your company, but at the very least it is important to outline the qualities you desire—beyond the basic duties of the job—and make these very clear to the HR department who can distinguish usually better than the entrepreneur which technical skills are needed. In Hess' *Grow to Greatness*, he emphasizes that hiring takes time and is hard, "Even though you hire the right person, that hiring requires the entrepreneur to focus on and manage the management team's personal dynamics. Getting managers to be good team players and engaging in constructive dialogue with each other takes work". (Hess, 2012, 262)[8] While it may seem like tedious work up front, hiring someone who is constantly unhappy and cannot get along with coworkers is like inviting a destructive disease into the office. Believe me, it's worth the effort.

Good hiring practices focus on how a candidate will fit into the company culture through multiple interviews, some more casual and out of the office. The key takeaway when it comes to hiring, though, is not to rush the process. It might feel like you need someone in that seat *now*, especially during rapid growth periods, but slowly hiring the right person is far more beneficial than getting just anyone's butt in the chair only to find out he's eating away at the culture you've worked so hard to develop.

THIS IS SUSTAINABLE—AND PROFITABLE—ENERGY

Exploring your feelings about your own past, extending grace rather than judgment to your employees, taking job candidates on social outings. this is all well and good, I hear you saying, but how do I make a profit?

Let's look back again at *Les Misérables*. In this beautiful story a priest embraced his Position of Opportunity in the life of Valjean, passing down a legacy of leadership. What did that priest gain? Well aside from the personal fulfillment and internal joy that comes with extending grace to another human being at the moment he most needs it, it's my assumption that the priest earned back more than the value of the silver Valjean took. Look again at how Valjean responded to the priest's act of mercy. He gave back with his life's work. And don't you think he gave back tenfold to the monastery over the course of his successful lifetime?

Are you an owner who would rather achieve immediate profit at the expense of the long-term dedication of good people? If so, your gain will be short lived. This world, so focused on community and relationships, no longer rewards the greedy boss who is out for themselves with no thought of helping others.

Once again, we can look to Southwest Airlines as an example. One of the many heroic acts immediately following 9/11 was how Southwest Airlines took care of their people by avoiding layoffs. The company was losing millions each day, but CEO Jim Parker made his priorities crystal clear when he said, "Clearly we can't continue to do this indefinitely, but we are willing to suffer some damage, even to our stock price to protect the jobs of our people" (Hoffer Gittell 2005, 242)[9].

This is a CEO who put his own needs (maintaining his stock prices and sustaining profits) behind those of his employees, who were likely terrified about what might happen on their next flight. He took care of his people and, in turn, his people took care of him through dedication, hard work, and trust. This kind of attitude and behavior will build organizational resilience and sustain a company's energy. When your people truly believe that you are more interested in fostering relationships with them than you are in raking in profits, they will extend you miles of grace, offer unfettered loyalty, and help you build the successful organization of your dreams where profits will soar.

The Dalai Lama was asked about what surprised him most regarding humanity. "Man, because he sacrifices his health in order to make money," he replied. "Then he sacrifices money to recuperate health. And then he is so anxious about the future that he does not enjoy the present; the result being that he does not live in the present or the future: he lives as if he is never going to die, and then dies having never really lived" (quote taken from Jeff Van Kooten Blog, January 23, 2014)[10]. Isn't it time that you replaced the old way of surviving life with a new way of enjoying life? If you take time to do these things in this chapter, you will find sustainable, passionate energy to wake up to each day.

If this is what you desire, I'd suggest you re-read the beginning of this chapter to refresh your memory of any material that made an internal connection or triggered certain feelings as you read. Even as I was reading this for the last edit, I thought to myself, I really need to read this book every so often to remind me of what's important. Not even the author will get it right all the time.

SUSTAINABLE ENERGY

((QUESTIONS TO CONSIDER))

1. How have your past hurts influenced your current leadership style?

2. What lies are robbing you of joy and a life of abundance?

3. Who do you need to forgive?

4. In what areas do you need more of an awareness of how you respond to others?

5. How can you affirm yourself and not sit in judgment once you acknowledge these areas?

6. What can understanding your own humanness teach you about your employees and how they can be led?

7. How can looking into what drives you encourage you to be a better leader?

8. What steps have you implemented to make sure you hire the right people for the company, not just for the job?

9. Do you need to take better care of your own health and the wellbeing of those around you.

((CHAPTER SIX))

THE EMERGENT LEADER

MY HOPE IS THAT THE DEFINITION OF THE TWENTY-FIRST-CENTURY, emergent leader is changing and beginning to unveil itself. But that change doesn't start with institutional mandates or updated manuals, it starts in the heart of each individual leader. You will be an amazing leader if you stop clinging to the notion that securing your own future is more important than fostering the growth and prosperity of those you lead. If you haven't already, begin to open yourself up to the truth that living an abundant life is just as much about pouring into the lives of others as it is receiving that energy for yourself.

There's been a lot to sort through up to this point. The fact that you've stuck with me even when what I've said isn't easy to read is a testament to your desire to lead in a way that breathes life into leadership. Here are three more clarifications of what this will look like:

CIVILITY

When I look around at this traditional climate, my first thought is that what we are lacking is civility. In its most basic definition, civility is politeness in speech and actions. But, it goes beyond that—a civil person actually wants to collaborate with different perspectives. Here's a definition from the Institute for Civility in Government's website, which I believe translates to the emerging leader as well:

> "Civility is claiming and caring for one's identity, needs, and beliefs without degrading someone else's in the process. Civility is about more than just politeness, although politeness is a necessary first step. It is about disagreeing without disrespect, seeking common ground as a starting point for dialogue about differences, listening past one's preconceptions, and teaching others to do the same. ... It is about negotiating interpersonal power such that everyone's voice is heard, and nobody's is ignored." ("What is Civility?", n.d.)[1]

Who could be a more amazing example of civility in leadership than the late Nelson Mandela? Who is more entitled to justified anger than one who is persecuted and falsely imprisoned? Yet, instead of allowing the trials of oppression and imprisonment to embitter him, Mandela chose forgiveness and genuine civility. Instead of wishing for the destruction of his oppressors, Mandela found a way to genuinely empower those around him to succeed and thrive. As the man himself said, "It is better to lead from behind and to put others in front, especially when you celebrate victory when nice things occur. You take the front line when there is danger. Then people will appreciate your leadership."(CNN.com, January 24, 2008)[2]

There is a wonderful philosophy that some of the Eastern cultures embrace that I believe would give us some guidance as to how to put this civil, emerging type of leadership into action. It is part of the shifting of thought that is necessary to maintain harmony amidst your daily life of leadership. Douglas Brooks, a scholar of philosophy and professor of religion at the University of Rochester, has broken down this philosophy into a tantra. Tantra is derived from the Sanskrit words *tanoti*, meaning expansion, and *trayati*, meaning liberation (*Wikipedia,* May 11, 2014, http://en.wikipedia.org/wiki/Tantras)[3]. Brooks presented three axioms during a virtual lecture for his online Rajanaka courses in January of 2014 that relate to his study of this Tantra. He spoke of three rotating statements that keep each other in balance and check: 1) I am not you, 2) I am something like you, and 3) I am nothing but you.[4]

If any one of these three takes precedence, the whole no longer exists in its completeness. For example, "I am not you" is part of the respect and autonomy each individual is given, but if taken

KAI-ZEN

alone, it becomes a narcissistic statement that would jeopardize the ability to make good choices for the whole group. Too little respect and autonomy, conversely, may lead to an individual being deceived and not being true to himself. The second statement, "I am something like you," conveys that we share in our humanness the same structure of eyes, ears, hands, etc., and that we are capable of encountering similar feelings and experiences. An overemphasis of this might lead to people pleasing at any cost that predisposes a person to make only feeling based decisions. Too little of this and we are plowing over others, ignoring their needs. "I am nothing but you," means that we actually see our humanity to the point of acting on behalf of others with their best interests in mind. Too much emphasis on this third point leads to over control, thinking for others without allowing them to bring their talents to the table. Too little, and you are apathetic, never able to trust anyone or be aware of what makes others tick.

While no one can perfectly balance these axioms, it is important to heed the wisdom that comes from asking yourself throughout any one day, "Am I leaning too heavily or too lightly on one of these Tantras? Is this causing a bias in my opinions or actions?"

Mandela was someone respected by the world being truly civil, which allowed the trials of prison to refine his position of authority and open him up over those years to the belief that the person guarding him was no different than he himself—this is the third tantra we just mentioned. Pondering within himself as he sat in the presence of his enemy for many years taught him in more ways than one, how to unify a people that once held great bitterness toward each other. Looking in the mirror to see his own humanity led him to forgive and look beyond his pain to collaborate both sides towards the middle. But, he had to be willing to be exposed. Mandela's humility to see past himself allowed him to progress to the next level of civility, which is having a desire for all groups around him to gain (Nicoli, *Nelson Mandela Centre of Memory,* Nelson Mandela's Warders).[5]

Another insight that Mandela understood was one of the most important ways to build community and camaraderie: he showed his enemies that, in their uniqueness, they were no different than the other side. Though just a sport, he found the ability to get both sides of this internal war to cheer for the same rugby team. This was brilliant! Notice that he made sure to require the South African National Rugby team to go to the front lines of slum areas and give coaching clinics. The players needed to meet these dear people and see that they had no right to believe that they were more valuable than any one of these kids. By the end of the day, they had built many meaningful relationships during those tours. It made the national team start to understand that they 1. We're not like them, 2. Yet, something like them, 3. And at the same time, nothing but them. What foresight on Mandela's part to unify a divided country into sharing equal values, leading to peace and prosperity (Invictus, 2009)[6].

You and I are not likely to encounter oppression on such a scale, but Mandela's actions and attitudes serve as a poignant example to all of us. Because we all are people, we all have pain. This pain cannot be compartmentalized outside of the workplace, but rather it stays with us wherever we go. Our pain can contribute to all sorts of breakdowns in communication with co-workers, teammates, and employees. Ask yourself: How can I put aside my past grudges or a sense of entitlement in order to become the kind of leader who looks at my employees as equals? How can I position myself as a leader rather than someone who's out for glory?

ALWAYS A STUDENT OF LIFE

Using power to have control will only come back to bite you. As a leader, you must learn to manage your position of power and authority. You do this by understanding that you, too, are a student. You have things to learn, and what you learn will ultimately benefit the whole. Each new bit of knowledge you acquire can be poured back into people, leading to peace and prosperity. When following this path, you might be pleasantly surprised to experience that you also are finding purpose and fulfillment.

Friedman's *New York Times* interview with Bock concludes with this quote from the Google vice president, "In an age when innovation is increasingly a group endeavor, it also cares about a lot of soft skills—leadership, humility, collaboration, adaptability, and loving to learn and re-learn. This will be true no matter where you go to work."[7]

We tend to overlook the importance of having a love of learning. By the way, I didn't say a love of accumulating knowledge, but rather it is an openness to learn from others and know that you can be a student of each person you meet. In an ever-changing world, there are so many things to discover—and rediscovered. Getting stuck in a rut of routine without embracing your growth as a person will wear out your zeal and passion to lead.

In his October 3, 2011, *New Yorker* article, "Coaching a Surgeon: What Makes Top Performers Better?" writer and surgeon, Dr. Atul Gawande, explored the need for coaching across professions—including in medicine—to improve skills and master new techniques, basically to stay sharp. Hiring an outside coach, while common among athletes and performers, is still almost unheard of in many professions. But Gawande, who brought in a retired general surgeon Robert Osteen to help sharpen his skills, asked a question in his article that I think is worth asking no matter your profession or position. "It will never be easy to submit to coaching, especially for those who are well along in their career," he wrote. "I'm ostensibly an expert. I'd finished long ago with the days of being tested and observed. I am supposed to be past needing such things. Why should I expose myself to scrutiny and fault-finding?"[7]

Osteen challenged Gawande in many ways. I was most impressed with the mentor's wisdom when he told Gawande, "Most surgery is done inside your head. Your performance is not determined by where you stand or where your elbow goes, it's determined by where you decide to stand, where you decide to put your elbow."[8]

In the workplace there are many applications to this enlightened form of leadership. This is exactly the kind of forethought you need as a leader. Just because you've risen to a position of authority doesn't mean leadership will always come naturally to you. Just because you are in charge doesn't mean you have earned the trust of those under you. To answer Gawande's question, often it takes exposing your weaknesses and accepting criticism in order to grow, develop, and improve. It takes accepting that you won't get it right much of the time at first, and being okay with that. It ultimately takes a person who loves to learn and re-learn.

BEING A SILENT LEADER

Leadership is like a rainbow. It's colors get clearer the less you strive to be the focus. If you start to pursue it for the position, it will elude you and be unobtainable. Another way to put this is, leadership is about standing in the raindrops (obstacles) under the rainbow in order to be the prism that allows light through you to refract the full spectrum of colors that each person's strength in the group is brought out brilliantly. When you allow yourself to manifest the light of others working together, there will bring success that shines as in the splendor of a rainbow. The focus is simply on bridging the team effort from point A to point B, not on how you shine as a leader. The bridge becomes the rainbow of success that all have participated to make happen. Yes, it is important to know that you, the leader, are in the unique—and often challenging—position to demonstrate how to manage the raindrops (the stress, mistakes, and even failures). You set the tone, not only in what you say, but also in your actions and your attitudes on a daily basis. Yet you refuse to have the focus be on you, and instead put it on the mission at hand, bridging point A to point B with a beautiful rainbow of people.

In the CBS television series, *Undercover Boss*, a company boss or CEO disguises himself and works among his employees to see what really goes on within the company. Often, he uncovers problems on the line, but many times he discovers his employees are good-hearted, hard-working people just trying to get by. The touching conclusion of each episode usually finds the boss gifting his employees with bonuses or promotions based on what he saw in the field. The lesson, typically, is that when the boss descends to the lowest levels of the company, he learns something valuable from his employees. Here is that need to get face-to-face with your employees—even those in the lowliest positions—because everyone, by nature of their very humanness, has something valuable to offer. But wait, let's take this a step farther than where the show takes it. Being a leader isn't to deign to descend to the lowly bowels of your organization, dip in a tow, and rise back up triumphant in your effort to mingle with the masses. In fact, in light of the rainbow analogy, this is that trap to make you believe you *are* the rainbow. A leader of depth enters willingly and whole-heartedly into relationship with her employees. There is a monumental difference between deigning to grace employees with your presence and quietly walking in the trenches or in the rain with them, dispersing their colors. Often, that difference is evident in the leader's lack of ego. As sixth century Chinese philosopher, Lao Zi, said, "A leader is best when people barely know he exists. When his work is done, his aim fulfilled, they will say, 'we did it ourselves.'"(Michael Shinagel The Language of Business Blog)[9]

In my journey of being a student of life, and in authoring this book, I found great insight in the documentary, *I Am* (2011)[10]. I believe the film gives viewers hope that our culture could be at a tipping point of understanding community and our connectedness. This only sets us up with a need for an emergent type of twenty-first century leader that embraces this type of culture. Filmmaker Tom Shadyac (2011) outlines this connection to life when he says in the film:

> "One of the fundamental laws of nature is that nothing in nature ever takes more than it needs to survive and thrive. When it does, it becomes subject to this law and dies off as unnatural. … We have a term for something in the body that takes more than its share to the detriment of everything else that surrounds it; we call it…cancer."

Shadyac is basically saying it is unnatural to gather for ourselves more than we need. An ancient Indian civilization that he researched believed someone who gathered more than necessary was actually mentally ill. No longer can we as a leader pride this independent, dog-eat-dog mentality, or have an attitude that glorifies the one who claws his way to the top at the expense of those around him. It does appear that we are beginning to shift from this behavior, as more and more leaders are making a change for the better. I do sense that leaders are beginning to understand and accept this silent type of leadership and all that it entails. Namely, anticipating employees' needs and making necessary adjustments to your leadership style and methods, even if it means humbling yourself in the process. My goal is to help each one of you embrace a philosophy of leadership that not only breathes life back into your organization, but also ultimately transforms you into an emergent, twenty-first-century leader who *wants* to make positive changes that reveal people's most vibrant colors. This is true success in and of itself.

THE EMERGENT LEADER

((A QUESTION TO CONSIDER))

In our twenty-first century film appreciative culture, there is an endearing moment for the character of Harry Potter in the film *Deathly Hallows Part II* 2011,[2] when he finally had the all-powerful position of holding the 'elder wand' after the ardent task of defeating the lord of darkness, Voldemort. It was never Harry's intent to flaunt or use this wand as a position of power for his own gain. He instead made the decision of 'civility in leadership' to break the wand. This showed in his leadership choice of how he wanted to continue being a 'student of life' instead of thinking he had mastered power for the position itself. Harry 'exemplified leadership quietly' with his desire to keep equality, knowing that he couldn't have done it without the teamwork of all the people around him. (2011 *The Deathly Hallows*) In other words, instead of exploiting his newfound triumph, Harry decides to demonstrate civility in leadership and breaks the wand himself. His desire to honor those who helped triumph over evil came in the reward of trust, sacrifice and commitment to each other that lasted a lifetime. Now in stillness of thought, what wand of power is in your leadership style that needs to be broken?

((CHAPTER SEVEN))
LEAVING A LEGACY OF LIFE

"IF YOUR ACTIONS INSPIRE OTHERS to dream more, learn more, do more, and become more, you are a leader." John Quincy Adams[1]

Your primary role as a leader is to cast a vision for those who follow you. What's more, you are charged with nurturing that vision; feeding it with energy, support, momentum, and encouragement. Leaders, who understand their position is not for mere self-indulgence, but for honor and trust, will keep at the forefront of their decision making the wellbeing of their people. A higher purpose is brought into the equation when you as a leader, enter into the circle of life. How you breathe life into those around you will actually in turn bring purpose and fulfillment into your life. This social anthropology in the business, non-profit, military, entertainment, and athletic realm cannot be absent when truly assessing how to maintain and energize any system of life that includes living and breathing human beings. What I am suggesting is to not give such disproportionate placement of the business pyramid, where the status of only a few is acknowledged as valuable. May we rise, as leaders, to respect our fellow man and leave a legacy that breathes life into people and, in the process, breathes energy back into us to sustain harmony.

Leadership and authority have ruthless reputations. We're told that if we go into the business world, we need to be tough, impenetrable, and thick skinned. We need to be brutal in our pursuit of wealth and power. We're told this is the only way to succeed. What lies! To tell ourselves that success is found in the merciless amassing of money and power (both of which can fade as quickly as they are gained) is not only destructive to those we step on to get ahead, in the end it will destroy the soul. Make no mistake, when your soul is fatally wounded, your business won't be far behind. This reminds me of a quote from author Lynne McTaggart. "Business is based on scarcity and competition so that we fashion our world in such a way where we are needing to be significant at someone else's expense" (quoted in I Am, 2011).

McTaggart reiterated this concept in an August 24, 2013 article she penned for PositiveNews.com. "Other than on the sports field, the competitive mindset is probably the greatest impediment to progress. The latest research shows that students, employees, managers, business owners, couples, and neighbors are happier, healthier, and far more productive when they work together in collaborative ways."[2]

LEAVING A LEGACY OF LIFE

Emergent leader, picture yourself as a great painter preparing to set brush to canvas. You don't start by squeezing paint directly from each tube haphazardly onto the canvas. Your work starts by carefully selecting just the right colors, tempering paint, and layering stroke after stroke onto the surface. In this analogy, your employees are the paint, each with rich, deep hues and pigments all their own. Some leaders may try to force employees to fit a certain mold or role—trying to make a green fit where clearly blue would be a better choice, or mixing too much black into a vibrant red, dulling its true potential. As a leader, it's your job to celebrate and develop diversity, using every color available to you in the right way until something beautiful begins to emerge. Innovative leaders allow their employees' true colors to shine. They foster confidence and encourage individuality, so employees themselves begin to trust that their own pigments are a vital part of the overall painting, however bright or dull they may seem.

History remembers the Renaissance as a golden age of invention, innovation, and leaps forward in the fields of science and art. From beautifully designed and decorated cathedrals to finely tuned navigational tools, it took believing that more was out there for artists and inventors to step into the unknown and discover what was missing. I'd like to suggest that we in the business world are in our own sort of Renaissance. This year, 2014, is the Chinese year of the horse, a year of enlightenment and good fortune. I would like to suggest that this, along with a challenging economy, is drawing people to invent a new way of life, a freer way of being that fills their lives with joy and a renewed purpose. This will ultimately bring a renewed sense of dignity in life, liberty, and peace for all. Here we are, in the year of the horse, standing square in the middle of an age of enlightenment, poised to significantly change how we view leadership. Perhaps Mahatma Gandhi said it best when he remarked, "I suppose leadership at one time meant muscles; but today it means getting along with people."

In chapter four I talked about Trilogy Health Services' president and CEO Randy Bufford. Bufford demonstrates just how much he gets this new style of leadership. For him, it starts not with a Type A personality or a hard driver who is willing to succeed at any cost, but with an attitude of humility. "We tell our managers that leadership is a learned business skill," he said. "It starts with somebody who's willing to humble themselves for the benefit of others. We work hard on humility… Overall, we've got a good culture of not having arrogance, and when I see it, I really emphasize that it can tear you down pretty quickly" (quoted in Hess 2012, 229)[3].

LEAVING A LEGACY OF LIFE

What motivates you? Think about it, when you wake up in the morning, what makes you excited to go in to work? Hopefully the answer isn't "I'm in it for the money." The excuse that money is all that someone cares about is exactly what wears a person down and causes misery. If you are feeling more like a martyr than a leader these days, or if you've just accepted anxiety, ulcers or heart palpitations as part of the job, I believe you're missing the key message of Kai-Zen. Humanizing the work place and any other form of organization will actually breathe life into you, the leader, and bring with it a better bill of health. How can you begin to turn your leadership into the kind that values each and every person for his or her uniqueness?

I believe that you who are reading this have already chosen to embrace Kai-Zen leadership. Once you start to understand this simple concept, the whole world opens up to you. The joy and completeness that this will bring to your heart and life is worth much more than the unstable stocks and bonds or the toys you may accumulate. Another benefit to leading with others in mind is that you can share in both the successes and setbacks. You have shoulders to lean on and an organization full of people in your corner. Successful owner of Room & Board, John Gabbert, understands that having engaged employees is what sets his company apart. Again, Hess (2012, 165)[4] quotes Gabbert as a prime example of growing to greatness. "I never wanted to be the biggest. I never thought about size. I just wanted to be the best and to spend my time at work with good people doing something more meaningful than just making money or keeping score."

It's an immense undertaking, but it starts with small choices. And the great thing is, you're not in it alone. The burden of reinventing your company lightens when you start to let go and trust those around you. Assuming you hired your staff because they are competent, creative, and qualified individuals, it's time to pass on your passion for reinventing your workplace and allow them to create new systems, come up with effervescent ideas, and be part of the process. Sure, it will take some work. Part of what is resurrecting the current leadership Renaissance is a new generation of workers who simply see the world differently. Free yourself from the co-dependent, fear-based mindset of the past and grab hold of the spirit of exploration and innovation that marks the future.

I would like to propose that at this time in history there is a wonderful tidal wave of opportunity for those who choose to ride the wave rather than stand still in its wake. It is an age of enlightenment, a level of consciousness that could bring a significant shift in how we view leadership. But even still, nothing ever is completely new under the sun. When I was visiting Sarasota, Florida

LEAVING A LEGACY OF LIFE

during the composing of this book, I had a yoga instructor, Randall, who was intentional in each practice he led. He mentioned for one of the sessions that in the ancient cultures of India there was a term, *sri* (pronounced shree). It's Sanskrit for the depth of 'more fullness'. "If we could only start to envision that there is so much more out there in the universe for us to learn and enjoy," Randall remarked. "Sri is a type of abundance that never runs out." Can you think of a better time to reach for more than you can imagine than at this very moment?

My final charge to you as a leader is this: start to think universally rather than remotely. When you get caught in a cycle of myopic thinking where the world revolves around your own survival, you're going to spin out of control. Be keenly aware of the consequences—positive and negative—that your attitudes, actions, and choices can have for those who work with you day in and day out. If and when you are able to open your eyes to another way of doing life that centers on communication, respect, humility, and appreciation, the possibilities for your people are limitless.

I can't help but leave you with one last anecdote of someone I have respected all of my life. Let me tell you about a leadership legend who went beyond civilized, beyond compassionate, to self-sacrificing in her leadership. They called Harriet Tubman the

KAI-ZEN

Moses of the Underground Railroad, and she left a true legacy of life through her work in the Civil War-era. She wasn't educated; she didn't have badges of honor or trophies on her mantel. What she did have was passion, drive, conviction, and the ultimate need to set people free—both physically and spiritually. She only used her position as leader to bring others to a better place. She taught others how to grow, believe, take chances, and reach their full potential. She came up with innovative ideas when obstacles tried to shut her down. At the expense of her own safety, she gave others the opportunity to live a life of freedom.

The leadership choices you make today can and will impact generations to come. Sure, you'll make mistakes, along with the rest of the world. Embrace them and use them to fuel compassion for others who will also mess up from time to time. Let your eyes open to another way of doing life, another way of setting your soul free to create an atmosphere of abundance and collaboration, that encourages communication within the walls, cultivating unimaginable capabilities.

Live in peace with yourself and with your fellow beings, knowing that this is the first day of the rest of your life.

NOW GO, AND LEAVE A LEGACY OF LIFE!

LEAVING A LEGACY OF LIFE

((QUESTIONS TO CONSIDER))

1. Have you painted a clear picture of your organization so employees can see what they are working towards?

2. In what ways has communication in your organization broken down?

3. Do your employees know their unique personhood and skills are what will make your organization a masterpiece?

4. Are you demanding them to think like you? If so, could there be another way to do it with their input?

5. How are you using (or underutilizing) each employee's unique strengths for the overall betterment of your organization?

6. What would a Renaissance look like at your company?

7. What truly motivates you to succeed?

8. Do you think your answer is hurting or helping your actual success?

KAI-ZEN

9. What do you hope your legacy of life will be?

((ACKNOWLEDGEMENTS))

To my best friend and husband, Brad – you are the love of my life.

To my kids, Hanna, Ingrid, Lars, Bria And Britta – nothing compares with being your mom.

To my dear friend, Sue – your prayers paved the way for this book.

To the dear people who have allowed their story to be shared and many who's stories weren't shared - I am honored to be a student of your experiences.

To my good friend, Monica – you believed in this book before I did.

To my editor, Sarah – you are a skilled word surgeon.

To my family and close friends – for your encouraging words, prayers and understanding when I went M.I.A. to finish the book.

To Lake Superior and the Gulf of Mexico - gazing at your beauty allowed my mind to clearly contemplate and freely write.

((BOOKMARK - CITATIONS))

CHAPTER ONE

1. Http://www.forbes.com/sites/joshbersin/2014/03/15/why-companies-fail-to-engage-todays-workforce-the-overwhelmed-employee/
2. Tom Rath and Jim Harter, *Well Being: The Five Essential Elements* (New York: Gallup Press, 2010), 133, 135.
3. Jody Hoffer Gittell, *The Southwest Airlines Way* (New York: McGraw-Hill, 2005), 13,19.
4. Kathy Rice, *The Pie Place Café'* (Duluth: Lake Superior Port Cities Inc. 2013), 121.

CHAPTER TWO

1. Http://www.olivetomato.com/food-and-eating-ancient-greece-vs-modern-greece/#ixzz2v6p89BMI
2. Roger Dow, Lisa Napolitano and Mike Pusateri, *The Trust Imperative: The Competitive Advantage of Trust-Based Businesses* (Chicago, IL: National Account Management Association, 1998), 182.
3. Lieutenant Colonel Joe Doty, Ph.D., U.S. Army, Retired, and Master Sergeant Jeff Fenlason, U.S. Army, "Narcissism and Toxic

Leaders", *Military Review*, January-February 2013, 55-60. http://usacac.army.mil/CAC2/MilitaryReview/Archives/English/MilitaryReview_20130228_art012.pdf

4. Www.npr.org/2014/01/06/259422776/arny-takes-on-its-own-toxic-leaders?se=tw&cc=share

5. Colonel Georg E, Reed, U.S. Army, Director of Command and Leadership Studies, U.S. Army War College (AWC), "Toxic Leadership", *Military Review*, July-August 2004, 67-71.

6. Army Doctrine Publication 6-22. *Army Leadership.* 2012, Washington, DC: Department of the Army.

7. Jim Collins, *Good to Great: Why Some Companies Make the Leap and Others Don't* (New York, NY: HarperCollins Publishers, Inc. 2001), 145.

8. Jody Hoffer Gittell, *The Southwest Airlines Way* (New York: McGraw-Hill, 2005), 116.

9. Hoffer Gittell, *The Southwest Airlines Way*, 117.

10. Hoffer Gittell, *The Southwest Airlines Way,* 119.

11. Http://money.cnn.com/magazines/fortune/best-companies/

12. Hoffer Gittell, *The Southwest Airlines Way* (New York: McGraw-Hill, 2005), 123.

13. Marianne Williamson, *A Return To Love: Reflections on the Principles of A Course in Miracles* (New York, NY: HarperCollins Publishers, 1992), 190.

CHAPTER THREE

1. Edward D. Hess, *Grow to Greatness: Smart Growth for Entrepreneurial Businesses* (Stanford, CA: Stanford University Press, 2012), 211.

2. Jon R. Katzenbach and Douglas K. Smith, *The Wisdom of Teams: Creating the High Performance Organization* (Boston, Mass.: Harvard Business School Press, 1993), 38.

3. Roger Dow, Lisa Napolitano and Mike Pusateri, *The Trust Imperative: The Competitive Advantage of Trust-Based Businesses* (Chicago, IL: National Account Management Association, 1998), 106.

4. Dow, Napolitano, Pusateri, *The Trust Imperative: The Competitive Advantage of Trust-Based Businesses*, 110.

5. Dow, Napolitano, Pusateri, *The Trust Imperative: The Competitive Advantage of Trust-Based Businesses*, 113.

6. Jane Dutton, *Energize Your Workplace: How to Create and Sustain High-Quality*

Connections at Work (San Francisco, CA: Jossey-Bass, 2003), 162,163.
7. Dutton, *Energize Your Workplace: How to Create and Sustain High-Quality Connections at Work*, 140-145.

CHAPTER FOUR
1. Michael P. Nichols, *The Lost Art of Listening: How Learning to Listen Can Improve Relationships* (New York, NY: The Guilford Press, 2009), 14.
2. Nichols, *The Lost Art of Listening: How Learning to Listen Can Improve Relationships*, 10.
3. Edward D. Hess, *Grow to Greatness: Smart Growth for Entrepreneurial Businesses* (Stanford, CA: Stanford University Press, 2012), 173.
4. Hess, *Grow to Greatness: Smart Growth for Entrepreneurial Businesses*, 175.
5. Jane Dutton, *Energize Your Workplace: How to Create and Sustain High-Quality Connections at Work* (San Francisco, CA: Jossey-Bass, 2003), 58.
6. Hess, *Grow to Greatness: Smart Growth for Entrepreneurial Businesses*, 356.
7. Roger Dow, Lisa Napolitano and Mike Pusateri, *The Trust Imperative: The Competitive Advantage of Trust-Based*

Businesses (Chicago, IL: National Account Management Association, 1998), 175.
8. Jane Dutton, *Energize Your Workplace: How to Create and Sustain High-Quality Connections at Work* (San Francisco, CA: Jossey-Bass, 2003), 163.
9. Atul Gawande, *The Checklist Manifesto: How to Get Things Right* (New York, NY: Henry Holt and Company, 2010), 66.
10. Gawande, *The Checklist Manifesto: How to Get Things Right,* 67.
11. Hess, *Grow to Greatness: Smart Growth for Entrepreneurial Businesses,* 235,236.
12. Jody Hoffer Gittell, *The Southwest Airlines Way* (New York: McGraw-Hill, 2005), 212.
13. http://us.greatrated.com/nestle-purina-petcare-company
14. Dutton, *Energize Your Workplace: How to Create and Sustain High-Quality Connections at Work,* 82.

CHAPTER FIVE
1. Matthew Kelly, *The Rhythm of Life: Living Every Day with Passion and Purpose*, (New York, NY: Beacon Publishing, Fireside Edition, 2004), 238.
2. Melody Beattie, *The Language of Letting Go*, (Center City, MN: Hazelden Foundation, 1990), 270.

3. Catherine Ponder, *The Dynamic Laws of Prosperity: Forces the Bring Riches to You*, (USA: BN Publishing, 2007), 69.

4. Esther and Jerry Hicks, *Sarah Book 1: The Foreverness of Friends of a Feather*, (Carlsbad, CA, London, Sydney, Johannesburg, Vancouver, Hong Kong, New Delhi: Hay House, Inc., 1995), 171.

5. Beattie, *The Language of Letting Go*, 97.

6. Thomas L. Friedman and Josh Haner, "How to Get a Job at Google", *NYTimes.com*, February 23, 2014, accessed February 23, 2014. http://mobile.nytimes.com/2014/02/23/opinion/sunday/friedman-how-to-get-a-job-at-google-.html?_r=0&referrer

7. Hicks, *Sarah Book 1: The Foreverness of Friends of a Feather*, 172,173.

8. Edward D. Hess, *Grow to Greatness: Smart Growth for Entrepreneurial Businesses* (Stanford, CA: Stanford University Press, 2012), 262.

9. Jody Hoffer Gittell, *The Southwest Airlines Way* (New York: McGraw-Hill, 2005), 242.

10. Vankooten, Jeff. n.d. "Powerful Quote from the Dalai Lama." *Jeff Vankooten* (blog). Accessed April 12, 2014.

http://jeffvankooten.com/2014/01/23/powerful-quote-from-the-dalai-lama/

CHAPTER SIX

1. "What Is Civility?" n.d. The Institute for Civility in Government. http://www.instituteforcivility.org/who-we-are/what-is-civility/
2. CNN.com/world, http://edition.cnn.com/2008/WORLD/africa/06/24/mandela.quotes/ January 24, 2008.
3. Wikipedia, May 11, 2014, http://en.Wikipedia.org/wiki/Tantras
4. Rajanaka Yoga: A Tantric Tradition of Auspicious Wisdom. Accessed January 11, 2014. http://www.raganaka.com/srividyalaya.html
5. Mike Nicoli, Nelson Mandela's Warders, Nelson Mandela Centre of Memory, http://www.nelsonmandela.org/content/page/nelson-mandelas-warders .
6. *Invictus*. 2009. Directed by Clint Eastwood, USA: Warner Bros. Pictures, DVD.
7. Thomas L. Friedman and Josh Haner, "How to Get a Job at Google", *NYTimes.com,* February 23, 2014.

8. Atul Gewande, "Coahing a Surgeon: What Makes Top Performers Better?" *The New Yorker*, October 3, 2011, accessed February 14, 2014.
9. Michael Shinagel, "The Paradox of Leadership", *Harvard Division of Continuing Education, The Language of Business* (blog), accessed April 24, 2014, http://www.dce.harvard.edu/professional/blog/paradox-leadership .
10. *I Am*, 2011, Directed by Tom Shadyac, USA: Shady Acres Productions, DVD. http://www.iamthedoc.com/thefilm/
11. *Deathly Hallows Part ll*. 2011. Directed by David Yates USA: Warner Bros Pictures, DVD.

CHAPTER SEVEN

1. Susan M. Heathfield, *Inspirational Quotes for Business and Work: Leadership*, http://humanresources.about.com/od/workrelationships/a/quotes_leaders.htm
2. Lynne McTaggart, *Positive News*: "From 'me' to 'we': the power of connection", August 24, 2013, accessed April 12th, 2014. http://positivenews.org.uk/2013/positive_perspective/13660/me-we-power-connection/#
3. Edward D. Hess, *Grow to Greatness: Smart Growth for Entrepreneurial Businesses*

(Stanford, CA: Stanford University Press, 2012), 229.
4. Hess, *Grow to Greatness: Smart Growth for Entrepreneurial Businesses,* 165.

((CONNECT WITH THE AUTHOR))

Whether you received *Kai-Zen: Breathing Life Into Leadership* as a gift, borrowed it from a friend or purchased it yourself, thank you for taking the time to read this book. Hopefully you are able to get a breath of fresh air towards your work place, enjoy the person that you are and then offer what you learned to another.

0 / 0 / 0 / 0 / 0 / 0

If you are interested in writing to the author to share one of your *Kai-Zen* stories, would like information about her speaking engagements or would like to invite her to speak at an event you are hosting, please address all correspondence to:

Kai-Zen Solutions LLC
14 Black Point Boulevard
Lutsen, MN 55612
United States of America

720-515-6205
E-mail: kaizenleadershipbook@gmail.com
www.Kai-ZenSolutions.com

CPSIA information can be obtained
at www.ICGtesting.com
Printed in the USA
FFOW03n0223021115
18222FF